The Annals of the Yeomanry Cavalry of Wiltshire

Henry Hope Graham

THE ANNALS

OF THE

YEOMANRY CAVALRY OF WILTSHIRE.

COLONEL G. T. J. SOTHERON-ESTCOURT
(LORD ESTCOURT).
1890-1898.

THE ANNALS

OF THE

YEOMANRY CAVALRY

OF WILTSHIRE.

VOL. II.

BEING A COMPLETE HISTORY

OF THE

PRINCE OF WALES' OWN ROYAL REGIMENT

FROM 1893 TO 1908.

BY

HENRY GRAHAM.

DEVIZES:

GEO. SIMPSON, "GAZETTE" PRINTING WORKS.

1908.

LIST OF ILLUSTRATIONS.

INDEX.

APPENDICES.

THE YEOMANRY CAVALRY OF WILTSHIRE.

CHAPTER XVII.

1885–1889.

DURING the autumn of 1884, a proposal had been made 1885
for the authorization by Her Majesty the Queen of a Table of Precedence for the several regiments of Yeomanry Cavalry in Great Britain, and after a considerable amount of correspondence between the War Office and the Colonels of the regiments, an experimental list was issued which gave the Ayrshire Regiment the first place, the Royal Wiltshire being the fifth on the roll.

But a subsequent, and fuller investigation of the various claims showed that the Wiltshire Regiment had clearly been raised before the others, and the Marquis of Bath embodied a detailed statement of the raising of his regiment in 1793 in a letter to the Secretary of State.

As in addition to other proofs this was supported by references to the *London Gazette*, the claim to the first place was recognised formally by the authorities, and a revised list issued. This is now officially printed in the Army List, and places the Royal Wiltshire in its proper position as the Senior Regiment of Yeomanry Cavalry in the Service.

Lord Bath received at the same time a letter, dated War Office, 27th Jan., 1885, saying:—The Secretary of State has now submitted to Her Majesty a Precedence Table of Yeomanry Cavalry Regiments, and the position allotted to the Wiltshire Yeomanry Cavalry is No. 1.

1885 Efforts were made afterwards by several of the other corps to controvert this position, notably by the Derbyshire Regiment, which asserted that it had been in existence for 200 years at the least. Now there is no doubt that there did exist from very early times mounted trained bands, which formed part of the militia. But these were most distinctly not Yeomanry Cavalry, the last being not Militia at all, but a purely volunteer force, which is now the only surviving portion of the volunteer cavalry, artillery, and infantry raised during the Napoleonic Wars. The other mounted militia bands seem to have died out during the early part of the 18th century.

It has already been shown, in the first chapter of these Annals, that the speech of Mr. Pitt on the 5th March, 1794, gives the first mention of the term "Yeomen Cavalry", and he distinctly alludes to them as a body to be raised in the future, and to be an *entirely new and original force.*

The plan for the augmentation of the land forces for home defence which was shortly afterwards sent round to the Lords Lieutenant of Counties again speaks of Yeomanry Cavalry as a new force, and distinguishes it both from the Militia and the Fencible Cavalry. If any confirmation of this argument were needed, it can be found in the fact that Mr. Sheridan, on the 24th March made the proposal of this plan the ground for denouncing the ministers for trying to raise troops without the consent of Parliament, thereby showing plainly that these Yeomen Cavalry could not possibly have previously existed, and Mr. Pitt had to agree to Sheridan's motion and to bring in a Bill to legalize his action in this matter.

But at any rate the dates of the granting of the Commissions in the *London Gazette* could not be controverted;

the Secretary of State declined to re-open the matter, and declared himself satisfied. 1885

Indeed the other corps did not themselves dispute the fact that the Wiltshire Regiment was the earliest raised of the new Yeomanry, but based their claims on the allegation that they had been in existence as Train Bands before 1794, and that this existence had been continuous, though under another name. A careful study of the subject by any impartial person will show that this alleged continuity has no possible basis of fact.

The regiment assembled in 1885 for Permanent Duty at Devizes on the 12th May. The total marching-in strength was 347 of all ranks; more than at the last training, and indeed the largest muster that there had been for many years. Colonel The Marquis of Bath was in command.

As H.R.H. The Duke of Cambridge, the Commander-in-Chief, had been pleased to signify his intention of inspecting the regiment in person, Colonel Mussenden, the Inspector-General of Auxiliary Cavalry held his own inspection on Saturday, the 16th.

On the following Monday the regiment was to have paraded at 10 a.m. in the Market Place, but several very heavy showers came on in succession, and the Troops were kept under cover till the last moment, when they paraded on the Green and thence marched to Roundway Down, getting wet through on the way. There were 360 of all ranks on parade, out of a total strength of 399.

The Commander-in-Chief, who travelled by special train from London with his staff, was received at the station by the Mayor and Corporation, who presented a short Address of welcome, and, attended by Colonel Brett, the officer commanding the Brigade District, rode through the town, which was prettily decorated with flags and loyal

1885 devices, straight up to the review ground, where he was received with the royal salute.

The ground was kept by the Bath Troop of the North Somerset Yeomanry Cavalry, assisted by the Devizes and Melksham Companies of North Wilts Rifles. There were a large number of spectators on the ground, among them being General Elkington, the Inspector General of Auxiliary Forces. The regiment paraded 352 of all ranks, and in spite of the wetting the men and horses had received presented a smart appearance. Indeed H.R.H. the Duke was pleased to remark at the time that he could see plainly that, though the rain had taken the polish off everything, that the greatest pains had been taken to ensure a smart turn-out, with the most creditable results.

The usual parade movements were gone through, followed by some field movements, and ending with dismounted practice, a charge and pursuit. The Troops then reformed on the Parade ground, and the line advanced in review order, halted, and gave the royal salute. His Royal Highness then addressed the regiment as follows:—

"Lord Bath, officers, non-commissioned officers, and men of the Royal Wiltshire Yeomanry Cavalry,—I have been extremely pleased by the inspection, and with this most excellent turn out of a very efficient yeomanry regiment. I have also been extremely pleased with the smartness of the regiment and with the cleanliness of the equipments. You are well mounted, your horses are in good condition, and very fairly trained for the purpose for which they are required; the men seem to understand their work, and the officers know how to lead them. I consider this corps a pattern corps, and well deserving the commendations I have heard passed upon it in other quarters. I believe the yeomanry of this country to be a most useful and valuable force, and I am glad to take an opportunity of occasionally coming and seeing for myself what they can do. I consider those I have seen very efficient, but of none that I have seen have I seen a regiment more efficient than you are. In fact I consider that this regiment led by you, Lord Bath, has done credit to you, to your brother officers, to your non-commissioned officers, and to your men; and I shall go back to London throughly satisfied, and I may say surprised, with the efficiency of everything that has come under my notice." 1885

Accompanied by Colonel the Marquis of Bath, the Duke then proceeded to a large tent on the Down where he had lunch with the officers and their friends.

Afterwards H.R.H. inspected the regular troops and the volunteers at the Le Marchant Barracks and returned to London later in the afternoon.

The officers gave a ball at the Assembly Rooms in the evening, and the next day the troops were dismissed.

This year regulations for the issue of good-conduct badges as a mark of "length and efficiency of service" were sanctioned by the Commanding Officer.

In 1886, the regiment assembled for Permanent Duty 1886
at Salisbury on Monday, 10th May, Colonel the Marquis of Bath being in command. The marching-in state showed a strength of 302 of all ranks. The weather was very bad during the whole week, and on the Thursday was so cold and wet that the troops did not parade till the afternoon. On Saturday afternoon a Military Tournament was held at the Butts, and as the rain kept off the sports proved very successful, though it was still very cold and windy. On the Tuesday following the regiment was inspected on Homington Down by the Inspector-General of Auxiliary Cavalry, Colonel E. Wood, C.B., in the presence of Lieut.-General Sir G. Willis, G.C.B., commanding the Southern

1886 District. The weather, fortunately, remained fine until after the parade movements had been gone through, though rain fell heavily during the march back to Salisbury. Both Colonel Wood and Sir George Willis expressed themselves well satisfied, and on the 18th May Lord Bath published the following order:—

Regimental order.—Colonel The Marquis of Bath has much pleasure in repeating in orders the terms in which Lieut.-General Sir George Willis, G.C.B., and Colonel E. A. Wood, C.B., Inspector of Auxiliary Cavalry, expressed themselves on the smartness of the regiment and its efficiency in the field. Lieut.-General Sir G. Willis said that it was the best Yeomanry regiment that he had seen, and he had inspected a great number. Colonel Wood declared himself astonished at the efficiency of the regiment, the smartness of the turn out, and the knowledge and intelligence displayed, both by the officers and men. Colonel The Marquis of Bath, in conveying the high approbation of these distinguished officers to the regiment, wishes to record his own thanks to both officers and men for the attention and zeal that have enabled the regiment to earn such credit under the trying circumstances of the weather during this Permanent Duty, these having been more unfavourable than any experienced by it during the past thirty years.

A ball was given by the officers in the Council Chamber in the evening, and on the following day the regiment was dismissed.

Martini carbines were issued this year, the Sniders being withdrawn.

1887 In 1887, the regiment assembled at Devizes on the 16th May. The marching-in state showed a total strength present of 328 of all ranks.

The Marquis of Bath was in command, but was called away in the evening owing to a very sad family bereavement, and Colonel Sotheron-Estcourt assumed command for the remainder of the training.

Out-post duty was performed on the 20th, and on the

following Tuesday the inspection was made by Colonel Wood, C.B., there being 303 of all ranks present out of a total strength of 370. 1887

The regiment was dismissed on the following day, the deep sympathy felt for Lord Bath by every member having had a most depressing effect during the entire training.

In 1888, the regiment met for Permanent Duty at 1888
Salisbury on Tuesday, the 8th May, Colonel The Marquis of Bath commanding. The marching-in state showed a very considerable reduction on the previous year, there being only 268 of all ranks on parade.

On the next day Major-General Ravenhill, Inspector-General of Army Remounts, attended the parade on Homington Down for the purpose of inspecting any horses that might be offered for sale by the yeomen for army purposes. Only twenty-five were offered, and of these only two were taken.

On the Friday following a Military Tournament was held at the Butts. The principal event, jumping by sections, was won by the Rood Ashton Troop after a stiff contest, the Malmesbury Troop running them very close.

On the Saturday the regiment was exercised in outpost duty, the "general idea" being that an enemy's force was advancing on Salisbury with the intention of destroying the railway.

Salisbury was occupied by three squadrons under Major Long, and the defending force was ordered to reconnoitre in the direction of Stonehenge, where the enemy was reported to have been seen the previous evening.

The "enemy" consisted of the second squadron under command of Captain Phipps.

Major Long moved his centre squadron, under Captain Lord F. B. Bruce, along the Devizes road, while the right

1888 squadron, under Lieutenant Helms, covered the advance, moving on the Stratford and Woodford roads, and the left squadron, under Major Neeld, on the Wilton and Stapleford roads.

Major Long reached the Druid's Head at 12.15, and, having received information that the enemy had been seen near Stonehenge, halted his force, and threw out a line of picquets, covering the ground from Wilsford on the right, by the Druid's Head, to Winterbourne Stoke on the left.

Captain Phipps, after an hour's skirmishing, detached Lieutenant Goddard with the Swindon Troop to make a demonstration against the centre, and he, finding the line opposed to him weak, managed to force his way through, and, reaching the Fisherton bridge, blew it up at 2.15 p.m. Captain Phipps, in the meantime, moved down into Winterbourne, which was held by a dismounted party under Lieutenant Fuller.

A sharp engagement followed, which ended by Captain Phipps' party being temporarily put out of action, in the course of which that officer was considerably damaged by being shot in the eye with a blank cartridge discharged at close quarters by an over-excited opponent.

While these events were progressing, Sir John Kelk and the Salisbury Troop had made a wide detour by Steeple Langford round Grovely Wood, and had reached Fisherton by the Wilton road, but only to find that the Swindon Troop had been beforehand with them. The rest of the troops then returned to quarters.

The regiment was inspected by Colonel Wood, C.B., on the following Wednesday, there being 277 of all ranks present out of a total of 339. Mr. Silas Taunton having kindly lent a large field, situated on the Devizes road, near the new Cut, the inspection parade was held there instead of at Homington Down. The ground was kept by the Salisbury and Wilton Companies of the Wiltshire Rifles. 1888

By order of the Inspector-General, the 4th squadron was sent on to occupy the parade ground, and to throw out picquets towards Salisbury. It was intended that the other three squadrons should make an attack, but, owing to the troops getting mixed up with the crowd of carriages and foot-people, so much confusion ensued that this manœuvre had to be abandoned. The usual parade movements, followed by a short field-day, were then gone through. The weather, though threatening, fortunately continued fine until the Inspection was over, though rain fell heavily immediately afterwards. The Inspecting Officer expressed himself well satisfied with the regiment, particularly with the quality of the troop-horses, which he said showed a continuous improvement year by year. The troops were dismissed the following day.

On the 1st July this year an Army Order was issued directing that no Yeoman should be enlisted under seventeen years of age or over forty-eight; and that, except in special cases, no Yeoman should be retained in the service after having attained fifty years of age.

In 1889 the regiment assembled for Permanent Duty at Swindon, for the first time in its history. There was no doubt that the reversion to the old plan of bringing the corps out in different towns year by year, instead of confining the training to Salisbury, had had a most favourable influence on recruiting, and it was decided to assemble this year at Swindon. 1889

The regiment received a most enthusiastic welcome from the townspeople when it marched in on Tuesday, May 21st. The whole town was decorated with flags and triumphal arches, and the road by which the troops were

1880 expected to arrive was lined with eager spectators. The Malmesbury Troop was the first to arrive, and was met by the band and the Swindon Troop, now nearly double the strength of last year's muster.

Colonel the Marquis of Bath was in command, but owing to ill-health he was unable to take an active part in the outdoor work, and the leadership in the field consequently devolved on Lieut.-Colonel Sotheron-Estcourt.

The marching-in state showed 265 present of all ranks. The regiment drilled in a large meadow at Medbourne Farm, Liddington, about 2½ miles from the town.

On the Saturday the regiment was exercised in outpost duty in conjunction with the North Wilts Rifles under the following "idea":—"A cavalry force, advancing from the west, throws out a line of outposts from Hackpen Barn to Four Mile Clump, covering its main body, which is engaged in collecting supplies from the surrounding country in Barbury Castle. At 2 p.m. an infantry force will arrive at Barbury to support the cavalry.

"Another cavalry force, advancing from the east by Ogbourne St. George, finds the enemy's cavalry in position in front of Barbury Castle. It therefore throws out a line of outposts from Coombe Hill by New Barn to the Marlborough and Barbury Road, and sends for reinforcements. On the arrival of his infantry by train at Ogbourne the commander of the Eastern force will attempt to capture Barbury Castle and the supplies there."

The Western force occupying Barbury, which was composed of two squadrons with four companies of the North Wilts Rifles, under command of Colonel Sotheron-Estcourt, took up the prescribed position at Barbury Castle, covered by a line of picquets and vedettes. At one o'clock the Eastern force of two squadrons under Captain Long, came into contact with the advance parties of the Western force on Coombe Hill, and after some reconnoitring halted, and threw out a line of picquets opposite it. At 3 p.m. the Eastern infantry, consisting of the four Swindon companies of the North Wilts Rifles, arrived at Ogbourne station, and having detrained, marched straight for Coombe Hill. 1889

The cavalry, having reformed, advanced from each flank upon Barbury Hill, but being received with a heavy fire from the infantry posted in the entrenchments, had to retire with the loss of a troop.

The Eastern infantry then deployed and advanced to the attack, but after a brisk engagement found the enemy too strongly posted, and had also to retire after losing nearly half their number.

There were several cavalry charges on either side, but owing to the number of spectators on the ground who greatly interfered with the movement of the troops, "cease fire" was sounded and the action terminated somewhat abruptly. The troops then reformed, and marched to a large meadow belonging to Mr. Kemble at the foot of the Downs, where Colonel Luce took command of the whole force. The troops then marched past, reformed line, and advanced in Review Order, finishing with a Royal Salute and three cheers for the Queen, in honour of Her Majesty's Birthday.

On the Monday a Military Tournament was held at the old Croft, and in the evening a Torchlight Procession and Carnival, which was organized by the Swindon Reception Committee, terminating with a bonfire and fireworks; and on the following evening a ball was given in the Corn Exchange.

On the Wednesday the regiment was inspected by Colonel E. Wood, C.B., at the drill ground, there being present 267 of all ranks out of a total of 316. Lieut.-Colonel Sotheron-Estcourt commanded in the field, as the

1889 Marquis of Bath, who was present as a spectator only, was not well enough to do so. Rain fell heavily during the greater part of the proceedings, and the march past had to be rather hastily performed in consequence.

The next day the troops were dismissed, having had every reason to be well satisfied with their first visit to Swindon and the welcome they had received from the citizens, for which the Reception Committee afterwards had a cordial letter of thanks from Lord Bath.

This year the rules for the competition of troops for sword exercise were altered. Twenty instead of twenty-four being to compete out of troops of forty or over, and sixteen men out of troops of less strength.

On the 9th October Captain Aylmer vacated his appointment, his five years' term of service having expired, and Captain H. J. Scobell, 2nd Dragoons (Scots Greys), was gazetted Adjutant in his place.

CHAPTER XVIII.

1890–1892.

In 1890 the regiment assembled for Permanent Duty at 1890
Devizes on May 8th, under Colonel the Marquis of Bath. The marching-in state showed a total of 243 of all ranks. The next day was very wet, but the usual drills on Roundway Down were gone through in spite of the weather. On the Saturday it cleared up and continued fine during the remainder of the training.

On the Tuesday following the regiment was exercised in out-post duty in conjunction with the Marlborough Cadets, the Devizes Companies of the North Wilts Rifles, and a company from the Brigade Depôt.

The "general idea" was that a besieged force in Devizes was in urgent need of provisions, and that an attempt was to be made to get a convoy into the town. The besiegers having received intelligence of this, dispatch a force of cavalry and infantry to intercept and capture the convoy.

The escort to the convoy which was under command of Major Neeld, consisted of the Rood Ashton, the Chippenham, and the Salisbury Troops, and 90 Marlborough Cadets under Captain Rundell. The intercepting force, commanded by Colonel Sotheron-Estcourt was made up of the remaining five Troops of the Yeomanry, the Devizes Volunteers and the Brigade Depôt Company.

Major Neeld managed to bring on a fight with the intercepting force while the convoy slipped away unperceived in another direction and succeeded in getting safely into the town, though Lord Bath, who acted as umpire,

1890 was of opinion that the escort would have been annihilated by the superior numbers of the opposing force.

The Regimental Sports were held on the Wednesday afternoon, the prize for Jumping by Sections being won again by the Rood Ashton Troop, Devizes being second.

Lieut.-General* Sir D. Drury Lowe, K.C.B., inspected the Regiment on Thursday the 15th, there being present 251 of all ranks out of a total strength of 293. The ground was kept by the Devizes Companies of the North Wilts Rifles. The inspecting officer expressed himself well satisfied, though he made some remarks about the low strength present, particularly that of the Salisbury Troop which only paraded thirteen members. The Troops were dismissed the following day.

During this Training, regulations were issued for the better performance of stable duties, which had a most beneficial effect on the condition of the horses.

In September a series of Cavalry Manœuvres was held in Berkshire, in the neighbourhood of Uffington, in which the Regiment took part.

Lord Bath not being able himself to attend, Lieut.-Colonel Sotheron-Estcourt took command of the detachment, which was made up of volunteers from the several troops, namely, Chippenham 17, Devizes 21, Swindon 28, Malmesbury 15, Marlborough 22, Salisbury 7, Rood Ashton 40, and Warminster 8. Total 16 officers, 8 permanent staff, and 134 rank and file. Captain Long acted as second in command, and Lieut. Goldney as regimental quartermaster, an office he filled with such zeal and ability that he earned the sincere gratitude of all ranks.

The troops were formed into three squadrons, 1st

* The post of Inspector of Auxiliary Cavalry was now abolished. All Yeomanry was inspected by the Inspector General of Cavalry, who was relieved of the Command of the Aldershot Cavalry Brigade.

Squadron, under Captain Lord F. B. Bruce, Marlborough 1890
and Swindon; 2nd under Major Neeld, Chippenham, Devizes and Malmesbury; 3rd under Lieut. Helme, Rood Ashton, Warminster, and Salisbury.

On the 13th September the troops marched into Uffington Camp, the Devizes and Marlborough Troops marching in independently, while the remainder, with the regimental staff, paraded at Swindon at 2 p.m. before marching. The three squadrons were attached to the 1st Cavalry Brigade under Major General Le Quesne, and took part in all the manœuvres that followed up to the 19th September, doing good service in the field, where they were usually given some special duty to perform. On one occasion they particularly distinguished themselves by a brilliant charge on the 12th Lancers, who were completely defeated with the loss of two squadrons placed out of action. Their scouting also gained much commendation, particularly on one day when they were temporarily attached to the Second Brigade.

On Tuesday the 16th, H.R.H. the Commander-in-Chief arrived and witnessed an engagement between the two opposing forces followed by a march past.

This fight consisted of an attack by the entire Cavalry Division on a skeleton enemy, according to a plan devised by Sir Evelyn Wood. At 9.30 a.m. the Division under command of General Sir Baker Russell was in the neighbourhood of Fawley, on the road southward from Wantage to Newbury, one battery of artillery, the Mounted Infantry—dismounted for the occasion—and sufficient officers and men to make up a skeleton division, lay nearer to Wantage under the command of Colonel French, 19th Hussars. This Division held a strong position on the heights just above and covering Wantage.

The attack by the remaining troops afforded a brilliant

1890 spectacle. The action resulted in the success of Sir Baker Russell, this being necessary in order that the whole force should get down into the low ground for a march past. The Commander-in-Chief, who was accompanied by Lord Wantage, Lord Wolseley, Sir Redvers Buller, and a large staff of officers, among whom were the French and American military attachés.

There was no royal salute at the commencement of the review, the troops starting at once at a walk, headed by the massed bands.

When the 3,400 mounted men present were drawn up on the broad plain they presented a magnificent spectacle. The Life Guards, Blues, and Dragoons had discarded their service tunics, and appeared in field-day order; the Household Cavalry had no cuirasses, but all wore brilliantly burnished helmets that flashed back the sunlight in rippling waves as they moved. The three strong squadrons of Household Cavalry were loudly cheered, as also were the 19th Hussars and 12th Lancers, who seemed to have found much favour with the Berkshire folk. A hearty cheer too was raised for the Wilts Yeomanry, and also for the scarlet-coated troopers of the Berkshire Regiment, who, however, were not so numerous as their brethren from Wiltshire.

By 2 p.m. all the troops were on their way back to camp. The total numbers on parade were 3,392 men, 3,315 horses, and 25 guns, including machine guns. Of the whole force only 31 men and 211 horses were returned sick.

At a luncheon given on the ground, H.R.H. the Duke of Cambridge acknowledged the great obligation of the army to the Berkshire landowners and farmers for so readily assisting the State in the way they had done. The Duke, who left Lockinge on the Wednesday following, issued an Army Order in which he stated that he was thoroughly satisfied with the manœuvres; that there had been an earnestness and military knowledge displayed by all ranks in every arm employed which was most gratifying, and which promised well for the future; and that the excellent condition of the horses at the march-past proved the care bestowed upon them by the commanding officers. H.R.H. also congratulated Sir Evelyn Wood and Sir Baker Russell upon the instructive and successful manner in which the manœuvres had been carried out. 1890

The squadrons marched out of camp on Saturday, the 20th September, and the Troops proceeded direct to their several head-quarters. During the week the Royal Wilts had fully sustained their usual high character both for smartness in the field and for good conduct in camp. The men subsisted on army rations, and the horses on forage as supplied to the regular troops. All the men messed together in one large marquee tent, provided by Sergeant Coles, of the Warminster Troop, who filled the office of caterer to the regiment. In the evenings smoking concerts were held, which were largely attended by the N.C.O.'s of the cavalry regiments of the First Brigade. The general health while in camp was exceedingly good, not a single case of serious illness being reported, with the exception of Sergt.-Major Peers, of the Devizes Troop. The Sergt.-Major had been in bad health for some time previously, and was sent home on the 16th, where he died three days later, to the deep regret of the whole regiment. With the exception of one or two sore backs, there were no casualties among the horses, and altogether on his return Colonel Sotheron-Estcourt was able to make a most favourable report to Lord Bath of the creditable manner in which the duties, both in camp and in the field, had been performed.

1890 On the 14th November this year, Colonel The Marquis of Bath, to the great regret of all ranks, resigned the command, which he had held since 1876, and received instead the appointment of Honorary Colonel. On the 15th November the following Regimental Order was issued:—"Lord Bath cannot permit himself to resign the active command of the regiment without addressing a few words to the officers, non-commissioned officers, and men of the Royal Wiltshire Yeomanry Cavalry.

"Lord Bath has had the privilege of being in command for more than fourteen years. During the last two years, however, he finds that additional calls on his time, combined with somewhat indifferent health, prevented him from devoting that amount of attention to regimental details which the responsibilities of command call for, and being strongly of opinion that the distinction of command should accompany its responsibilities, he thought it right to retire.

"Lord Bath wishes to make known to the regiment the very great regret he experienced in finding himself compelled to take this step." Lord Bath then went on to thank all ranks for their loyal support in maintaining the high reputation of the regiment, and concluded with saying that he felt sure that it would stand by his successor as it had done by him, and that he felt the greatest confidence that in Lieut.-Colonel Sotheron-Estcourt's hands it would sustain in the future the high character of the past. Lieut.-Colonel Sotheron-Estcourt was promoted to the command in the same *Gazette*.

1891 In 1891, the regiment assembled for Permanent Duty on Tuesday, May 26th, at Marlborough, for the first time since 1874, Lieut.-Colonel Sotheron-Estcourt being in command. The marching-in state showed 244 of all ranks on parade.

The regiment drilled on the Common. On Friday the 1891 29th, a field-day was held in Savernake Forest under the following "General Idea":—

"An invading force having managed to land a Division at Weymouth sends on an advance guard with orders to occupy Salisbury and to push out strong advance parties of cavalry and infantry in the direction of London. These parties have orders to capture small towns and villages, and to hold them until reinforced. Information having been received that Marlborough is the object of attack of one of these parties, orders are sent to the officer commanding the Wilts Yeomanry to drive them back."

Each force consisted of two squadrons with a company of the Marlborough College Cadet Corps attached, the invaders having in addition the College Cyclist Corps.

This last paraded at 10 a.m., and having marched out to Puthall threw out a line of scouts towards Eight Walks. A strong patrol was placed on the right flank which proceeded as far as the Ruins, where it captured Sir John Kelk and two troopers. Another gallant officer only just managed to escape after a headlong gallop, which is reported to have covered several miles before he mustered up sufficient courage to pull up.

Meanwhile the Cyclists had been directed to advance with caution along the Salisbury road on the left, but meeting with some of the hostile cavalry they were brought to bay and nearly annihilated. Their shattered remains shortly afterwards encountered a fresh troop which captured them *en masse*, and they remained prisoners for the remainder of the action.

After a good deal of skirmishing in the forest, the whole of the two forces met at the Eight Walks, and a fight ensued in which the defenders were decided by the umpires to be victorious. The troops then reformed, after having partaken of a lunch kindly provided by Lord F.

1891 B. Bruce, marched past Colonel Sotheron-Estcourt and returned to quarters.

On the Saturday following, the Regimental Sports were held at Manton Grange. The Lloyd-Lindsay prize was won by the Chippenham Troop.

On Wednesday, the 3rd of June, the regiment was inspected by General Keith-Fraser, C.B., I.-G. of Cavalry, there being 244 present out of a total strength of 310. The ground was kept by the Berkshire Yeomanry Cavalry and the Marlborough Company of the Wiltshire Rifles. The next day the troops were dismissed.

Previous to the training this year a detachment was raised at Hartham by Sir John Dickson-Poynder. This was attached to the Chippenham Troop, which was henceforward generally styled the Chippenham and Hartham Troop, though its title was not officially altered.

1892 In 1892 the regiment assembled at Salisbury on Monday, May 9th, under command of Lieut.-Colonel Sotheron-Estcourt. The marching-in state showed a strength of 244 of all ranks. There was some difficulty this year in securing the usual drill ground at Homington owing to the Coombe Valley Cricket Club having leased the ground and laid down a pitch. Eventually the matter was settled by paying an extra £5 to the cricket club in addition to the usual £10.

On Thursday evening H.R.H. the Duke of Connaught, G. O. C. Southern District, arrived at Salisbury for the purpose of inspecting the regiment. His Royal Highness dined with the officers at the White Hart Hotel, but owing to the recent death of H.R.H. the Duke of Clarence he did not attend the ball given at the Council Chamber in the evening.

On Friday morning the regiment paraded in field-day

order at Homington for inspection. After the usual 1892
parade movements had been gone through, followed by some field movements, the squadrons were formed up in quarter-column and the Duke addressed them.

H.R.H. said he should not like to leave the parade without expressing his satisfaction at what he had witnessed. It was some years since he had seen an Yeomanry regiment which showed so marked an improvement as theirs; he thought, considering that it was only their fourth parade, that the movements were carried out with quietness, with considerable accuracy, and with great intelligence. He was very pleased to see the regiment so well mounted and so well commanded, and he thought they might look forward to keeping their centenary next year with the knowledge that the credit of the regiment had not only been maintained but improved on since it was formed. His inspection that day had been only that of the General Commanding the District, not that of a cavalry officer who held an annual inspection, but he could tell them with perfect honesty that the report he should have to make, the annual report he sent in of every regiment of the Southern District, would be a very satisfactory one to them. He was happy to think that the regiment was in such a satisfactory state. He congratulated them on being forty stronger than last year, and hoped that on the celebration of their centenary next year they would turn out the strongest muster that they ever remembered. H.R.H. concluded by thanking Colonel Sotheron-Estcourt for the parade.

After Colonel Sotheron-Estcourt had briefly expressed his acknowledgments, the Duke returned to Salisbury, and left for Portsmouth. The total strength present on parade was 249.

On the Tuesday following the regiment was inspected

1892 by Lieut.-Colonel Lord Beaumont, 20th Hussars, there being 280 of all ranks on parade, the ground being kept by the South Wilts Rifles. On the next day the troops were dismissed. The weather was very fine during the week, though cold.

CHAPTER XIX.

The Centenary of the Regiment.

1893.

This year 1893 being the anniversary of the hundredth year since the raising of the Regiment, great preparations were made for celebrating the Centenary at Devizes, where the Corps was enrolled on the 4th June, 1794—this very interesting event being rendered all the more worthy of commemoration by the circumstance of the Royal Wiltshire being the first regiment of Yeomanry Cavalry ever raised in England. H.R.H. the Prince of Wales signified his intention of honouring the regiment that bore his name by inspecting it in person on this memorable occasion. 1893

The Troops marched into Devizes on Thursday, May 18th, the marching-in state showing a total strength of all ranks of 306. The only officer not present was Lieut. Sir John Dickson-Poynder, who was suffering from a severe attack of influenza.

The town was decorated throughout with great taste, and a most lavish display of flags and illuminations in honour both of the Centenary and of the visit of the Prince of Wales. The whole of the main thoroughfares were lined with venetian masts; a fine castellated arch was erected at the entrance to the town, near the Assize Court; and a similar one by Southbroom Church; another was erected near the Bear Hotel on which was inscribed the names of the first officers of the Regiment and those of the present ones, and which was surmounted by various

1893 figures showing the uniforms of several periods, with the regimental motto above, *Primus in Armis.*

Drill went on daily as usual on Roundway Down: on the Sunday the Regiment attended Divine Service at the Parish Church, and afterwards was entertained at lunch by the Mayor, who was requested by Colonel Sotheron-Estcourt to convey the thanks of the Regiment to the people of Devizes for the welcome they had given to it.

After drill on Monday the Regimental Sports were held on the Down, the Jumping by Sections prize being won by the Chippenham Troop, Rood Ashton being second. On Wednesday the 24th May H.R.H. the Prince of Wales arrived for the purpose of reviewing the Regiment. During the morning there was a very large influx of visitors to the town, the railway alone bringing 6,000 excursionists from all parts of the County. The station itself was suitably decorated under the superintendance of Inspector Dickinson. The booking office was converted into a temporary reception room and the walls fronting the arrival platform were covered with crimson baize ornamented with gold fringe, the Royal Arms being displayed above the doorway, while flags and festoons of flowers and evergreens decorated all parts of the building. The royal train was timed to leave Paddington at 10.20 a.m., and running down without a stop was due at Devizes at 12.15 p.m.

From half-past eleven o'clock the precincts of the station and the whole line of the route by which the Royal procession was to pass was a scene of the greatest animation and excitement. Every possible provision had been made for the accommodation of spectators. In the Market Place the space surrounding the old monument had been railed off, and in other parts of the town many private individuals had erected stands for the use of the public. On

the banks overlooking the station quite an amphitheatre 1893
of spectators was formed, and as the time for the arrival of the Prince drew nearer the enthusiasm that prevailed was most marked.

A company from the Depôt, under Major Inglis, formed the Guard of Honour at the station itself, and the streets through Northgate Street to the Market Place were lined by the 3rd Battalion Wiltshire Regiment under command of Lieut.-Colonel Bennett. On the platform to receive the Prince were the Marquis of Bath, Hon. Colonel of the Regiment, Lieut.-Colonel Sotheron-Estcourt, Captain and Adjutant Scobell, Colonel Collingwood, commanding the 62nd Regimental District, and Colonel Codrington, 3rd Wilts Regiment.

At a quarter-past twelve the train entered the station. On stepping on to the platform His Royal Highness shook hands with Lord Bath, and afterwards with the other officers present. H.R.H. was attended by two equerries, Colonel Stanley-Clarke and Captain Holford, 1st Life Guards. Major Colston's carriage, drawn by four horses with two postillions, was in waiting, and as the Prince entered it, the Band outside the Station played the National Anthem and the populace burst into a roar of cheering. The seat next the Prince was occupied by Lord Bath, and the two equerries in waiting were on the opposite side. The escort consisted of 22 rank and file of the Royal Wilts, drawn from each troop of the regiment, the Devizes Troop providing 12 out of the number in honour of its being the first to be raised, under Captain Gwatkin, Lieut. Viscount Weymouth, and Quarter-Master Deacon. As the procession passed the Assize Courts, amidst continuous cheering, "God Bless the Prince of Wales" was sung by 1,000 children who were placed inside the yard.

His Royal Highness proceeded amidst the most

1893 enthusiastic demonstrations of loyalty to the headquarters of the regiment at the Bear Hotel, in the Market Place, where the 2nd Wilts Rifles under Captain Picot formed a Guard of Honour.

After the Royal Salute, the Mayor of Devizes advanced to meet the Prince as he reached the steps of the Inn, and asked H.R.H. to accept the humble address of the Corporation. The address, which was enclosed in a walnut casket with silver mountings, was as follows:—

"To His Royal Highness the Prince of Wales:—May it please your Royal Highness:—We, the Mayor, Aldermen, and Burgesses of the Royal Borough of Devizes, in Common Council assembled, beg to offer to your Royal Highness a respectful and hearty welcome to this ancient and loyal borough. We desire also to express our particular satisfaction at the fact that your Royal Highness's visit is made in connection with the celebration of the Centenary of a regiment which has the honour to be called 'The Prince of Wales' Own', and which while it is the oldest regiment of Yeomanry Cavalry enrolled in the United Kingdom, has, ever since it was first raised, been closely connected with this borough."

His Royal Highness handed to the Mayor a written reply, as follows:—

"Mr. Mayor and Gentlemen,—I thank you for your address, and I can assure you that it gives me much pleasure to have this opportunity of visiting your ancient and historical town. It afforded me great satisfaction to find myself able to comply with Colonel Sotheron-Estcourt's request, that on the occasion of the celebration of its Centenary I would inspect the corps which bears my name, and which was the first regiment of Yeomanry that was enrolled in the United Kingdom I wish every prosperity to your borough, and I trust that the close connection that has existed for so many years between Devizes and the 'Prince of Wales' Own' may long continue to the mutual advantage of both."

There was a renewed outburst of cheers as the Prince entered the Inn, where His Royal Highness was entertained at luncheon by the officers of the regiment.

After lunch the Prince of Wales proceeded to Roundway Down, where the review of the Yeomanry was to take place at 3 p.m. His Royal Highness mounted his charger at Mr. Coward's farm at the bottom of the hill leading up to the Downs. The ground was kept by the Royal Gloucester Hussars, under Major Sir Gerald Codrington and Captain Sir Perry Pole, together with the 3rd Wilts Regiment and the 2nd Wilts Rifles. An open space was left, into the centre of which the Prince rode, passing the standard of the Royal Wilts, which was held by a trooper of the regiment, and the Royal Salute was given as soon as His Royal Highness rode up. 1893

Accompanying the Prince were the Marquis of Bath, Hon. Colonel of the Wilts Yeomanry Cavalry and Lord Lieutenant, Colonel the Marquis of Worcester, Colonel Stanley-Clarke, who acted as *aide-de-camp*, Captain Holford, Sir Francis Grenfell, Adjutant-General for Auxiliary Cavalry, Colonel Salis-Swabe, commanding the 28th Regimental District, Major the Earl of Lonsdale, of the Westmoreland and Cumberland Yeomanry Cavalry, Major Long, Lieut. Viscount Weymouth, and Major Colston.

The total strength on parade was 301 of all ranks, the officers commanding the several troops being Major Sir A. Neeld, Chippenham; Captain Gwatkin, Devizes; Captain Goddard, Swindon; Major Sir H. Bruce Meux, Malmesbury; Major Lord F. Brudenell-Bruce, Marlborough; Captain Sir J. Kelk, Salisbury; Captain B. Helme, Rood Ashton; and Major C. N. P. Phipps, Warminster.

After the Royal Salute had been given, the regiment marched past by squadrons, ranked past by sections, and trotted past by squadrons, after which the sword exercise was performed. The line was then reformed, and advancing at the gallop up to the passing line, halted, and gave the Royal Salute. The Prince then addressed Colonel

1893 Sotheron-Estcourt, saying that he was very much pleased with the regiment, and with the march-past and the other movements, all of which had been done steadily and well. H.R.H. added that he would not address the regiment unless Colonel Sotheron-Estcourt particularly wished it, but would ask him to convey to it the satisfaction with which he had inspected the troops and seen them at their work.

His Royal Highness then rode off the ground and returned to Devizes, arriving at the Station at 5.30 p.m., attended by Lord Bath, Major Long, Major Colston, and other officers, and a few minutes afterwards left for London.

The general arrangements for the review were excellent, and everything passed off most satisfactorily. In the evening, by permission of Colonel Merriman, the band of the 2nd Wilts Rifles played a selection of music in the Market Place. A carnival was held at night, and the town illuminated, prizes being offered by the local Committee for the best car, the best historical character, the best comic character; and the best decorated and illuminated house. The proceedings terminated with a display of fireworks in Southbroom Park.

The following Regimental Order was issued after the review:—

"The Commanding Officer has been desired by H.R.H. the Prince of Wales to make known to all ranks the pleasure he experienced in inspecting the regiment to-day. H.R.H. was pleased to say he considered the turn-out and appearance of the regiment very good, that the parade movements were very well done, and the field movements carried out smartly and steadily. H.R.H. expressly desired the Commanding Officer to have his remarks published in the Regimental Orders, and he has the greatest pleasure in doing so."

On Thursday a Ball was given in the Town Hall at which H.R.H. the Duke of Connaught was present. On the Friday following the regiment was inspected by General Keith-Frazer, I.-G. of Cavalry, and the next day the troops were dismissed. 1893

Thus ended the Hundredth Anniversary of the raising of the Royal Wiltshire Yeomanry Cavalry, the first to be enrolled in England. Everything during the training passed off in the most satisfactory manner, and the weather on the whole was very favourable. The town of Devizes did all that could be done in honour of the occasion, and it was generally agreed that though perhaps not so strong as on some other trainings, the regiment was never better horsed, better turned out, or better prepared, to maintain its well-deserved and honourable reputation.

APPENDIX TO CHAPTER XIX.

THE CENTENARY MUSTER ROLL, 1893.

STAFF.

Hon. Colonel The MARQUIS OF BATH.
Lieut.-Colonel Commanding and Hon. Colonel G. SOTHERON-ESTCOURT.
Major and Second in Command, W. H. LONG.
Adjutant-Captain H. J. SCOBELL.
Surgeon-Lieut. G. T. K. MAURICE.
Veterinary Surgeon-Lieut. F. P. BENNETT.

"A" TROOP
(The Chippenham and Hartham).

Captain Sir ALGERNON W. NEELD, Bart (Hon. Major) Commanding.
Captain G. P. GOLDNEY (Hon. Major).
Lieut. J. M. FULLER.
Lieut. Sir J DICKSON-POYNDER, Bart.

Sergeant-Major A. Lawrence
Quartermaster W. Freegard
Sergeant J. H. Hiscocks
„ F. Hiscocks
„ R. Smith
Farrier-Sergeant H. Marchant
Corporal T. Bryant
„ C. Daniell
„ W. Church
„ J. B. Warrilow
„ F. Austin
Trumpeter J. Exton
Trooper B. Attwood
„ W. Baker
„ H. E. Banks
„ H. A. Banks
„ S. Bennett
Trooper W. Besant
„ T. Blackman
„ R. W. Bolter
„ W. J. Browning
„ G. Butler
„ A. Bence
„ J. Carpenter
„ W Clark
„ W. Coward
„ C. Duck
„ R. Flint
„ C. W. Fry
„ H. M. Godwin
„ W. Harry
„ C. T. Hawkins
„ R. S. Heath
„ G. N. Hobbs

"A" TROOP—*continued.*

Trooper C. Ind
„ W. Ind
„ J. R. Keevil
„ F. W. Lane
„ W. T. Lewis
„ A. Little
„ A. Maidment
„ A. Marsh
„ A. Mathews
„ J. Ogg
„ W Perrett

Trooper G. Purnell
„ T. Rumming
„ J. Sage
„ H. Sage
„ J. Theobald
„ J. Vines
„ F. W. White
„ J. Wilshire
„ W. J. Wright
„ H. Whitting

"B" TROOP

(Devizes).

Captain R. G. Gwatkin.

Lieut. Sir T. Fowler, Bart.

Lieut. J. F. Stancomb.

Sergeant-Major H. Bagshawe
Quartermaster Cole
Sergeant T. Ford
„ J. Nutland
„ D. King
Farrier-Sergeant T. J. Neate
Corporal C. Giddings
„ H. Romaine
„ W. Sudweeks
Trumpeter J. Pethett
Trooper J. Bidmead
„ R. Blair
„ H. Blencowe
„ J. Brett
„ T. Brookes
„ A. Burbage
„ H. Burry
„ W. Butler
„ T. Craxton

Trooper R. W. Dowse
„ R. Edwards
„ T. Flooks
„ F. Franks
„ H. Gundry
„ F. Hambly
„ J. Hunt
„ W. Hunt
„ H. W. Hutchins
„ W. Jolliffe
„ E. Lewis
„ C. Phipp
„ E. Price
„ R. Ruddle
„ M. Sloper
„ W. Turner
„ J. Tyler
„ W. Wilshire

"C" TROOP
(Swindon).

Captain F. P. Goddard.
Lieut. J. Joicey.

Sergeant-Major J. Holland
Quartermaster T. H Deacon
Sergeant H. Pakeman
„ W. Sloper
„ J. K. Smith
Farrier-Sergeant F. Hazell
Trumpeter J. Batten
Corporal C Fox
„ J. B. Godwin
„ N. Cook
Trooper C. Atsill
„ R. Atsill
„ F. Baily
„ A. Balch
„ E. Bendrey
„ F. J. Bush
„ H. T. Clifford
„ S. Coleman
„ F Dark
„ G. Elliott
„ R. B. Evans
„ C. R. Fox
„ J. Fulton
„ C. Godwin
„ J. Green
„ W. Green
„ T. Greenman
„ R Gregory
„ J. Hollyoak
Trooper T. Horsell
„ F. Kempster
„ P. Kernick
„ W. Keylock
„ T. King
„ H. Morris
„ H. Passmore
„ S. C. Sennard
„ W. Sheppard
„ E. Thomas
„ T. Townsend
„ J. Townsend
„ G. Tranter
„ F. D. Turner

Band.

Bandmaster E Lay
Sergeant E. Davis
Trooper K. Appleyard
„ R. Chivers
„ E. Clarke
„ J. Eatwell
„ B. Gilbert
„ G. Harding
„ T. Jones
„ J. Mayfield
„ R. Rider
„ H. Webb
„ J. Woodward

"D" TROOP
(Malmesbury).

Captain Sir Henry Bruce Meux, Bart
Lieut. A. E. Miles.
Lieut. A. G. Sutton.

"D" TROOP—*continued.*

Sergeant-Major F. Carpenter
Quartermaster W. Iles
Sergeant — Godwin
„ J. Moore
„ J. Tew
Corporal W. Collingbourne
„ J. Garlick
„ J. Reynolds
Trumpeter T. Jones
Trooper G. Alexander
„ G. Beavan
„ T. Bowles
„ M. Carter
„ F. Cole
„ — Day
„ H. Freegard

Trooper R. Greenhill
„ H. Iles
„ R. Jeffries
„ D. Jones
„ C Knapp
„ W. Mathews
„ H. Nicholls
„ N. Ody
„ A. Price
„ W. Reeves
„ A. Renwick
„ W Rich
„ E. Slade
„ H. Sutton
„ F. Tuck

"E" TROOP
(Marlborough).

Captain Lord Frederick Charles Brudenel-Bruce (Hon. Major).

Lieut. T. R. Curtis.

Sergeant-Major A. Creed
Quartermaster H. Woolcott
Sergeant T. Cole
„ B. Vines
„ C. Edwards
Corporal C. Clark
„ H. Collins
„ E. Smallbones
Trooper A. Bennett
„ H. Berry
„ J B. Burry
„ E. Butler
„ J. Caswell
„ J. Cole

Trooper J. Berry
„ J Duck
„ C. Edwards
„ G. Fall
„ J. Harding
„ J. B. Hillier
„ R. Hill
„ J. Hallick
„ J. Kingston
„ J. Looker
„ R. Long
„ S. Norris
„ H. Rawlings
„ G. Shire

"F" TROOP
(Salisbury).

Captain Sir JOHN KELK, Bart.
Lieut. J. BENETT-STANFORD.
Lieut. R. A. POORE.
Sergeant-Major Simons (Regimental Sergeant-Major).

Quartermaster J. Nutbeam
Sergeant F. Herring
„ H. Woods
Corporal C. M. Brown
„ J. Roper
Trooper T. Airs
„ M. Braithwaite
„ H Curtis
„ S. Dennis
„ E. Field
Trooper G. Ford
„ G. George
„ T. Grierson
„ F. Highman
„ T. W Jennings
„ H. Moore
„ H. Northover
„ J. R. Roe
„ C. Wallbridge

"G" TROOP
(Rood Ashton).

Captain BURCHALL HELME.
Lieut. G. L. PALMER.
Lieut. H. L. LOPES.

Sergeant-Major E. Morel
Quartermaster J. Collett
Sergeant J. E. Ashby
„ T. Candy
„ G. Pinchin
Farrier W. Cook
Corporal D. Bathard
„ F. Golledge
„ W. Hunt
„ E. Wake
Trooper J. Axford
„ U. Beavan
„ G. Brown
„ — Butler
„ F. Collins
„ — Davis
„ E. Ellis
Trooper G. England
„ H. Giles
„ J. Giles
„ W. Greenhill
„ F. Griffin
„ J. Hampton
„ S. Homan
„ A. Mathews
„ W. Milsom
„ J. Oram
„ C. Overton
„ A. Pike
„ H. Pike
„ — Reid
„ F. Rogers
„ T. Rogers
„ W. Ruddle

"G" TROOP—*continued.*

Trooper T. Rumming
„ T. Rogers
„ J. Shepherd
„ H. Sims
„ G. Slade
„ H. Taylor
Trooper E Tucker
„ J. Tucker
„ W. Tucker
„ H. White
„ W. Woodman
„ G. Woods

"H" TROOP
(Warminster).

Captain C. N. P. PHIPPS.
Lieut. Viscount WEYMOUTH.

Sergt.-Major F. Bartholomew
Quartermaster E. Parrot
Sergeant G. Chinn
„ W. Fulford
„ G. Gunning
Corporal E. J. Butcher
„ R. E. Coles
„ E. Pickford
Trooper E. Baker
„ G. Brown
„ G. C. Brown
„ C. Collier
„ A Dufosee
Trooper A. Foreman
„ A. Fry
„ W. J. Hall
„ H. Hooper
„ J. Hulbert
„ J. Jones
„ A. King
„ W. Marshman
„ W. Noad
„ B. Osborne
„ R Osborne
„ G. Price
„ J. Singer

CHAPTER XX.

1894–1898.

1894 In 1894 the regiment assembled at Swindon for permanent duty, on the 15th May, Colonel Sotheron-Estcourt being in command, and was inspected on the 23rd by Colonel Salis-Schwabe, the officer commanding the Bristol Regimental District. The weather was wet and cold during the training, and very bad on the inspection day. There were present on parade 269 of all ranks, including 21 officers, out of a total strength of 307.

On the 24th May the Rood Ashton Squadron proceeded to Cheltenham, to keep the ground at the inspection of the Gloucester Hussars by H.R.H. The Duke of Cambridge.

On the 9th of October Captain Scobell's period of service as Adjutant came to an end, though he was not gazetted out till the 11th November, when he rejoined the Scots Greys.

The following Order had been published previously, at the termination of the training, on the 23rd May, by Colonel Estcourt:—

"The Commanding Officer desires to express in Orders his hearty appreciation of the services which have been rendered to the regiment by Captain Scobell during the five years of his Adjutancy, and the regret with which he, in common with the officers, non-commissioned officers, and men of the regiment, view the approaching termination of his services with the Royal Wiltshire Yeomanry."

The good results of the increased attention of the Yeomanry Cavalry to musketry were this year plainly manifested, a very marked improvement being shown by all the regiments, and nowhere more than in Wiltshire. This year, six out of the eight troops scored a full attendance at musketry practice, and the other two troops only showed five absentees between them. In five troops there were no third-class shots at all, and in the remaining three together only six. 1885

The Marlborough Troop made the best average, though the Regimental Challenge Cup, which was shot for at Malmesbury, was won by Sergeant Ashby, of the Rood Ashton Troop. Colonel Paton, the Chief Instructor of the Hythe School of Musketry, highly commended the shooting of the whole of the Yeomanry Cavalry in his annual Report, pointing out that in the firing standing at 200 yards, there were only two Yeomanry regiments that did not score more points than the men of the Regular Cavalry.

No appointment was made to the regimental Adjutancy on Captain Scobell's vacating that post, but Captain Wyndham-Quin, the Adjutant of the Gloucester Hussars, was appointed Adjutant to the Brigade, and performed the duty for the two regiments in common during the remainder of his term.

In 1895 the training was held at Cheltenham, in conjunction with that of the Gloucester Hussars. The two regiments formed the 3rd Yeomanry Brigade, and it was generally felt that some experience of combined work was desirable. 1895

The two regiments assembled at Cheltenham on the 15th May, Colonel Sotheron-Estcourt being in command of the Royal Wiltshire, while Colonel the Marquis of Worcester, as senior officer, was in command of the Brigade. The regiments drilled at Prestbury, separately, for the first part of the day, and then together, when Brigade movements were practised.

The Brigade was inspected on the 23rd May by Colonel Gough, Assistant-Inspector-General of Cavalry, and dismissed on the 24th, after a most successful training, the

1895 weather having been all that could be desired. The regiment had the further satisfaction of providing the winner of the Brigade Prize for sword exercise in the person of Sergeant Ashby, of the Rood Ashton Troop. There were present at the inspection 270 of all ranks, out of a total of 301, the establishment being now 327. In July this year Captain Wyndham-Quin's term of service expired, and Captain Charles Bishop, of the 9th Lancers, was appointed Brigade Adjutant from the 1st of the month.

1896 In 1896 the regiment met for Permanent Duty at Devizes on May 21st, Colonel Sotheron-Estcourt in command, and Captain Bishop, Adjutant, and was inspected on the 29th by Colonel Dickson, C.B., there being 236 of all ranks present out of a total strength of 307.

Martini-Metford carbines were issued to the regiment this year in exchange for the Martini's.

In April 1896, the regiment had the misfortune to lose the Honorary Colonel, the Marquis of Bath, who died on the 20th of that month.

Lord Bath obtained his first commission in the Royal Wiltshire in 1850, and commanded from 1876 until 1890, when he found it necessary to exchange the active command for the less onerous duties of Honorary Colonel.

The Royal Wiltshire owed much to Lord Bath's constant and unwearied attention to its well-being during his long period of service with it. His cheerful and conscientious performance, indeed, of the very numerous and onerous duties entailed by his position, and his tactful kindness in fulfilling these, caused his loss to be greatly felt and lamented, both by the regiment and the county, as well as by his many friends of all ranks of life elsewhere. The funeral was attended by Colonels Estcourt and Long as representatives of the regiment.

On the 24th February, 1897, the Marquis of Lansdowne was gazetted Honorary Colonel of the regiment, *vice* the Marquis of Bath, deceased. Lord Lansdowne had been previously in the regiment, having commanded the Chippenham Troop from 1865 to 1873, when his political duties compelled him to resign. 1897

On the 13th May a squadron, under command of Lord Frederick B. Bruce, proceeded to Cheltenham in order to keep the ground for the Gloucester Hussars at their inspection by H.R.H. the Prince of Wales.

The training took place at Swindon, the regiment marching in on 19th May, Colonel Sotheron-Estcourt being in command. The inspection, which was made by Major-General the Honourable R. Talbot, C.B., the Inspector-General of Cavalry, extended over two days, the 26th and 27th, the former being devoted to a rather severe examination in various outpost duties.

There were present 243 of all ranks, out of a total strength of only 287, this being the lowest number the corps had mustered for seventy years.

The 20th June this year was the 60th anniversary of the accession of Her Majesty Queen Victoria, whose reign was now the longest in English history. This event, known as the Diamond Jubliee, was celebrated by great rejoicings throughout the country. Her Majesty made a state procession through London to St. Paul's Cathedral, the route being lined by troops throughout. Detachments representing most of the Yeomanry Cavalry regiments of Great Britain had the honour of taking part in the procession. The Royal Wiltshire detachment consisted of one N.C.O. and twelve troopers, under command of Major A. W. Neeld. The men were quartered at the Devon Hotel, London Road, Paddington. On Tuesday, the 22nd May, the detachment marched to the Horse Guards Parade

1897 in St. James' Park, and, with the Gloucester Hussars, were posted along the Mall, facing Marlborough House.

After the Royal procession had passed, the detachment marched back to their quarters, and on the following morning returned home.

The whole proceedings of this impressive ceremony passed off in a most satisfactory manner, without the least hitch, amidst indescribable enthusiasm. Upwards of 45,000 troops took part in it, either in the procession itself, or lining the route, there being present 4,500 Cavalry of the Line, 2,300 Artillery with 110 guns, 18,000 Infantry of the Line, 5,300 Militia, 500 Yeomanry Cavalry, 11,000 Volunteers, and 1,000 representing detachments from the Colonial Forces. The Diamond Jubilee was also celebrated throughout the County of Wiltshire on Sunday, the 20th, by special services at all the churches and chapels. The several Troops attended these, under their officers, in the parish churches of their respective headquarters.

This year the "squadron system" was nominally introduced in the Yeomanry Cavalry, with the object, apparently, of economising an Adjutant for every 2 corps, and 4 Sergeant-Majors of the Permanent Staff per regiment. The regiment was accordingly formed into three squadrons: A, Chippenham; B, Savernake; C, Rood Ashton. Three Sergeant-Majors were discharged: Bagshawe, Carpenter, and Morel, immediately after permanent duty; and one, Creed, notified for discharge as soon as he should have completed his 21 years' service. The payment and accounts of the Permanent Staff were transferred to Gloucester after Captain Scobell retired. The headquarters were transferred from Salisbury to Chippenham.

1898 On the 8th March, 1898, Colonel Sotheron-Estcourt relinquished the command, greatly to the regret of all

THE RIGHT HONBLE. W. H. LONG.
Colonel 1898-1906.

ranks, and retired from the service, and on the 23rd Major 1898
and Hon. Lieut.-Colonel W. H. Long was gazetted Lieut.-Colonel to command in his place.

Colonel Estcourt, on resigning, issued the following Order, dated 8th March :—

"Colonel Sotheron-Estcourt desires to express in Orders the very sincere regret with which he parts from the regiment as its Commanding Officer. From officers, non-commissioned officers, and from men alike he has unfailingly received all the support, consideration, friendly feeling and obedience to discipline that he could possibly have desired, and in laying down the honourable post, which he has held for eight years, he asks the regiment, each and every member of it, to accept his sincere thanks.

"Having had the privilege of serving as an officer in it for 37 years, he is able with satisfaction to remember that the regiment, both as regards officers and men, has been throughout essentially a County Regiment, composed of Wiltshire men, a bond of union greatly tending, in his view, to the well-being and spirit of comradeship so desirable in a regiment of Yeomanry.

"He has had the good fortune twice to take part with the regiment in manœuvres in conjunction with the regular forces, one on Salisbury Plain in 1872, and again on the Berkshire Downs in 1890; he trusts that the experience the regiment then acquired may shortly be renewed under the command of his successor.

"With every feeling of esteem and friendship he bids the regiment a most respectful farewell."

The following order was published by Lieut.-Colonel W. H. Long after his own gazette to the command :—

"In making the accompanying announcement the Commanding Officer wishes to express on behalf of the whole regiment, the great sorrow that is felt at the retirement of Colonel Sotheron-Estcourt, during whose period of command so much has been done to improve the efficiency of the Royal Wilts, and who, by his unfailing courtesy and kindness, has endeared himself to every member of the regiment."

This year the regiment assembled for permanent duty at Devizes, on the 26th May. It was inspected by Major

1898 General Sir G. Luck on the 2nd June, there being present 267 of all ranks, out of a total strength of 296. On the following day a second inspection was made by Field-Marshal Viscount Wolseley, the Commander-in-Chief, who was attended by General Sir J. Davis, commanding the Southern District, and Major-General Kelly-Kenny, Inspector-General of Auxiliary Forces.

On June 9th the following Regimental Order was issued:—

"The Commanding Officer has much pleasure in publishing the accompanying Order, which reflects great credit on all ranks.

"The Commander-in-Chief desires to express his satisfaction with his inspection of the Royal Wiltshire Yeomanry Cavalry. It is evident that the regiment is ably commanded, and that the Officer Commanding is ably supported by all ranks. The 'turn out' was satisfactory, and the horses are of a good useful stamp; and the men know how to ride them.

"The Commander-in-Chief commends the intelligent manner in which the outpost line was occupied, and the excellent way in which the various exercises were performed, particularly the dismounted work.

"*(Signed)* T. K.-Kenny,

"Inspector-General Auxiliary Forces.

"Devizes, 3 June, 1898."

It was decided this year to hold another great series of military manœuvres in South Wilts. These were arranged to take place in September, and the regiment, though unable to turn out a second time in the year as a whole, volunteered to find two squadrons for a part of the time.

However, the greater part of the regiment did turn out, to the number of 13 officers and 220 men, and these were ordered to join the Red, or Northern, Army on the 5th September.

CHAPTER XXI.

The Manœuvres of 1898.

The Manœuvres Act, passed in 1897, came into force on 1898 the 15th August. On the 16th the Southern Army began to assemble at Wareham, and on the 18th the Northern Army on Salisbury Plain. The Cavalry Division was concentrated at Bulford, under General Luck, for some independent exercise, but on the 29th it was divided into two Brigades, the first, or Aldershot Brigade, under Major-General the Hon. R. Talbot, being posted to the Northern, the 2nd Brigade, under Major-General French, to the Southern Army. Each Army consisted of an Army Corps of three Divisions, a Cavalry Brigade, and the usual corps troops, making up for the Northern force, which was commanded by H.R.H. the Duke of Connaught, a total of about 27,000 officers and men of all arms, with 97 guns, and 29 machine guns; and for the Southern Army, under Sir Redvers Buller, 26,700 men, 88 guns, and 31 machine guns. The Northern Divisions were numbered 1st, 2nd, 3rd, the Southern Divisions 4th, 5th, and 6th. Sir Evelyn Wood acted as Chief Director, with his headquarters at Chilmark, while the Umpire Camp was located at Fovant. The War Office being unequal to the task of providing either transport or food, these departments were leased to private contractors, Messrs. Whiteley & Co. being responsible for the former, and Lipton & Co. for the latter.

The "general idea" was complicated by the usual "imaginary" Armies so dear to the staff officer; but neither side appears to have paid much attention to these, and the manœuvres practically resulted in a Southern Army being supposed to have landed in the neighbourhood

1898 of Weymouth and marching on London, opposed by a Northern Force concentrated about Salisbury.

Each Army Corps went through a variety of separate field-days while the concentration was proceeding, but on September 1st the manœuvres proper began. The disposition of the two Army Corps was as follows:—

The Northern or Red Army had the 1st Division at Wilton, the 2nd and 3rd at Homington, the Corps troops at Winterbourne Ford, and the Cavalry Brigade at Bowerchalke. The whole of the Southern or Blue Army was concentrated at Blandford.

1st September. The Red Army received orders to move towards Shaftesbury, while the Cavalry Brigade was to reconnoitre as far as Blandford. The Blue Army was to remain at Blandford, while its Cavalry was to reconnoitre towards Salisbury; the intention being to bring off an engagement between the two Cavalry Brigades.

Red accordingly moved the 1st Division to Teffont, the 2nd to Fovant, and the 3rd to West Farm. The result of the day's fighting consisted merely of a number of small outpost combats, and an indecisive Cavalry action at Cranbourne Chase.

September 2nd. On the second day Red was ordered to occupy Charlton Down and take up a position to prevent Blue's advance on Salisbury, while Blue was ordered to carry this position at any cost. The 1st Division, on the right of Red's line, was directed to occupy a position from Melbury Hill to Compton Down, prolonging the line as far eastward as possible, the 2nd Division to work to the south of the 1st, and the 3rd to occupy Wingreen.

But the Blues had already seized Melbury Hill, so the 1st Division took up the line Charlton Down, Breeze Hill; the 2nd Division occupied Wingreen, the 3rd being placed in rear of the left in echelon.

The action began at 9 a.m., when Buller moved the 1898
4th Division to Tarrant Gunville, the 5th along the Blandford-Shaftesbury Road, and the 6th *via* Iwerne-minster to Laycombe Down, while his Cavalry Brigade forestalled Red by occupying Melbury Hill.

The result was a brisk attack on Red's position, Blue's principal force being directed against the 2nd Division at Wingreen. "Cease fire" sounded at noon, and Red was declared the victor, on the ground that his position was too strong to be forced. The two armies then fell back to the same camps they had occupied during the previous night.

September 3rd. Red's outposts now held the line Gillingham, Shaftesbury, Berwick St. John. His orders were to remain in observation of Blue, and to fall back on Fovant if attacked.

Blue's outpost line extended from East Stowe, through Melbury Abbas to Tollard Royal. His orders were to advance and drive Red eastwards.

The Director-General at first objected strongly to the orders issued by the Red commander on the ground that they were not likely to lead to an engagement, and though some alteration in them was made, his prevision was justified, as by the time Blue reached the limits assigned to the day's manœuvres Red had disappeared altogether.

The 4th September being Sunday, both sides rested in their respective camps.

September 5th. The "imaginary armies" now began to take part in the game, and both sides were informed that another Blue Army had landed at Bristol, being now at Bath *en route* for Devizes. Red was accordingly ordered to prevent the two Blue forces from joining hands, and with that view to operate about Codford and generally to maintain his hold of the line of the Wylye River; while

1898 Blue was told that he was to seize the Wylye, but that Red meant to attack him while on the march.

In consequence of the fiasco on the last day, the umpires were determined to bring off a fight this time. But with this intention they placed the two forces so close at the beginning of the operations that any reconnoitring was impossible, and the opposing Cavalry met at once in close formation. The Red Cavalry attempting to secure the western edge of Stockton Wood found the Blue Cavalry already there. A fight at once ensued. The Blue Cavalry charged the head of the Red's 2nd Infantry Division, who were in column, causing some loss and much confusion, but were in turn charged, while retiring, by the Blue Cavalry. Red's 2nd Division eventually occupied Stockton Wood after some further desultory and indecisive Cavalry encounters. But things generally had by this time got into such a state of confusion that at 11 o'clock the umpire-in-chief sounded "cease fire", and the day's operations came to a premature end.

The P. W. O. joined the Northern Army this day, and were sent into camp at Ford, near Salisbury.

The two armies had by this time got back to the same ground that had been fought over in the great manœuvres of 1872, and the actions on the following days somewhat resembled those fought at their close.

September 6th. An imaginary Red Army was now served out to the Northern Commander, who was ordered to cover a position supposed to be in course of preparation for it between Beacon Hill and Laverstock.

Red was accordingly instructed to take up a position with a rear guard of one Division, the 1st, between Yarnborough Castle and the Wylye, keeping the main body in reserve ready to support it.

The 1st Division, less one Brigade, took up the position

assigned to it early in the morning, with the Cavalry Brigade and the two corps batteries of Horse Artillery at Stony Hill in support. The P. W. O. was attached to the Cavalry Brigade, and ordered to occupy and hold the bridge over the river at Winterbourne Stoke, so as to secure the retreat of the rear guard if necessary. Red's main army was disposed on a line extending from Longbarrow Cross Roads to the 18th milestone of the Sarum-Devizes road. 1898

Blue was ordered to move east and seize the line of the river from Winterbourne Stoke to Berwick St. John, and bivouac near it. The Blue divisions were ordered to move as follows:—

5th Division from Chitterne St. Mary to Maddington.

6th Division E. Codford Down to Maddington.

4th Division from Codford to Claypit Hill.

Cavalry Brigade to Yarnborough Castle.

The infantry fight was preceded by some smart cavalry work on both sides, the reconnoitring of the Red Cavalry being particularly good. This culminated in a vigorous attack of the Blue Brigade on the Red guns on Stony Hill, which were put out of action in consequence. But the Red Brigade coming up at a gallop, caught the Blue Cavalry in flank while riding over the guns, and they in their turn had to retire discomfited; meanwhile the Red guns achieved the feat of putting the Blue balloon out of action.

The Blue commander now being convinced that Red's main force was at Yarnborough, concentrated his whole strength for an attack on that position, but before his dispositions were completed Red withdrew his rear guard across the river and retired on his main body, covered by the fire of the whole of his guns.

7th September. The operations of the seventh and last day of the manœuvres were intended to illustrate the

1898 crossing of a river in face of an enemy. Red was therefore ordered to force the passage of the Avon between Amesbury and Old Sarum; to attack the enemy, and to push him back West of the Salisbury-Winterbourne Stoke road.

Red's outpost line at the commencement of the day's operations was on the line Sarum High Post, No. 5 mile stone, Amesbury Road. His Cavalry Brigade was ordered to secure the bridges between Upper Woodford and Avon.

The 1st Division occupied the line of the Avon from Woodford to Avon Bridge.

The 2nd Division was directed on the Fords at Manor House and Lake House.

The 3rd Division and one brigade of the 1st Division on Mill Hill and Normanton. The reserves were placed between Salterton Down and Down Barn.

Blue's 5th Division was ordered to defend the line of the river from Little Amesbury to Woodford, 3½ miles.

The 6th Division watched the river from Woodford to Old Sarum, 2 miles.

The Corps Cavalry was ordered to reconnoitre to the south east.

Two squadrons and some Engineers were detailed to blow up Durnford bridge, and a half company of mounted infantry and 2 machine guns were posted to cover the ford at Normanton.

The 4th Division, the corps artillery, and the Cavalry Brigade were held in reserve at the Druid's Head, while the balloon was fixed at Boreland Hill. The morning, however, was very foggy, which prevented General Buller from deriving much benefit from this last, and the fog generally proved of considerable assistance to the Red Commander, who, having decided on his plans, proceeded to carry them out without reference to the dispositions of his adversary, who was not able to perceive his movements 1898 until the day became clearer with the rising sun.

Red ordered the 1st Division to cross at Heale House, the 2nd Division at the fords at Manor House and Lake House, and the 3rd Division, reinforced by a Brigade from the 1st Division, was directed to hold the high ground along the east side of the river, from Salterton to Avon Bridge, until the other Divisions were safely across. The corps artillery was posted on the high ground near High Post to cover the advance.

The action commenced by a dash of the Cavalry Brigade to seize the bridges and fords, the P. W. O. being on the extreme right of the line at Netton. The line of the river here was found to be already in the hands of Blue's advance parties, and the two squadrons were forced to retire. One squadron was then detailed to escort the guns, which were hurriedly brought up to support the attack, while the other succeeded, after a short fight, in seizing the bridge at Netton, which it held successfully for the rest of the day.

Meanwhile the remainder of the Cavalry Brigade was engaged in the attempt to seize and occupy the other bridges and fords south of Amesbury. Woodford bridge was successfully blown up by Blue. The 15th Hussars got the bridge at Heale House, and the leading company of the 1st Division crossed; but Blue attacked the head of the column so vigorously that it was forced to retire, and the bridge was destroyed to prevent the Blue cavalry crossing by it, and Red's Cavalry Brigade eventually retired and concentrated at High Post, leaving the infantry Divisions to continue the fight by themselves.

Favoured by the fog, Red managed to throw the 1st and 2nd Divisions across the river, and, pivoting on the left, these were swinging round to attack the left flank of

1898 the Blue defence, while a Brigade of the 3rd Division was in the act of crossing when the "cease fire" sounded. Blue, however, though unable to prevent the actual passage of the river, was firmly holding his right, while his two Divisions, supported by his corps artillery and Cavalry Brigade, were advantageously posted to withstand Red's attack on his left, which was rapidly being reinforced from his reserves. When, at noon, the "cease fire" was sounded, there had been but little actual fighting by the infantry on either side, though the artillery of each army, finding splendid positions on the high ground bordering the valley, had thundered across it without ceasing from the commencement of the action. The result of the day was accordingly given as indecisive, and both armies amicably crossed the Avon, and camping together near Beacon Hill, prepared for the grand March Past that was to bring the manœuvres to a close on the following day. The P. W. O. was now brigaded with the 2nd Dragoon Guards as the corps cavalry to the Red Army.

September 8th. Both armies combined were reviewed by the Commander-in-Chief, Field-Marshal Viscount Wolseley. The total force that marched past was 53,600 officers and men, 9,456 horses, 242 guns, and 486 waggons.

The day was fine, and the parade was a great success, the P. W. O. in particular receiving many compliments. The *Times* correspondent stated in his account in that newspaper:—

> "The Wilts Yeomanry took part throughout with the cavalry, and they have every reason to be proud of the way in which they acquitted themselves in this distinctly trying ordeal."

and the Commander-in-Chief stated, in the last conference held after the close of the operations, that "he noticed with great pleasure the way in which the Yeomanry rode and worked."

The general opinion, however, was that these manœuvres had been somewhat of a failure. The "cease fire" seemed invariably to have been sounded at the most interesting and important stage of each day's operations. The armies were too close together at the commencement of each action, the "ideas" were confused and complicated, though in effect they were for the most part ignored by both Commanders, and the cessation of the "state of war" every afternoon imparted a general air of unreality to everything. 1898

The experiment of entrusting the transport and supply departments to civilian contractors also proved by no means a success, though probably the soldiers came off quite as well as they would have done had the War Office undertaken these duties with the means that were then available. The P. W. O., at any rate, had no reason to bless the contractors, as their individual wants certainly were very badly catered for during the first two days they were out.

CHAPTER XXII.

1899.

1899 THOUGH the year 1899 was destined to see the commencement of the Boer War in South Africa, there were very few people in the country who either anticipated the complete rupture of the negotiations that had been entered into between the Colonial Office and Mr. Kruger, or who realized in the least the serious nature of the crisis that was so rapidly approaching.

The regiment this year made a fresh departure, and assembled for Permanent Duty at Weymouth in conjunction with the Dorset Yeomanry. The regiments, however, did not drill together, and the only time they met in the field was when they took opposite sides in the practice of outpost duty.

The regiment marched in on the 18th May. The 24th being the eightieth birthday of Her Majesty the Queen, the Commanding Officer, Colonel W. H. Long, sent the following telegram to Windsor Castle:—

"Your Majesty's Premier Yeomanry Regiment, the Royal Wilts, assembled at Weymouth, ask leave to approach your Majesty and offer on this auspicious day their tribute of loyalty and devotion to your Majesty's throne and person."

To this Her Majesty was graciously pleased to reply:—

"The Queen thanks you and all ranks of the Premier Regiment of Yeomanry for their kind message of loyal congratulations received to-day."

The regiment was inspected by Major-General French, who made a more than usually favourable report, on the 26th May, there being present 268 of all ranks out of a total strength of 292, and was dismissed on the following day.

On the 21st October the Salisbury and Warminster Troops provided an escort for H.R.H. the Prince of Wales, from Iwerne to Semley Station, the former sending 8 and the latter 18 rank and file, and on the 14th November another escort of 12 men, under Lieutenant Spencer, comprised of 1 sergeant and 6 men from the Malmesbury, and 6 men from the Chippenham Troop, attended H.R.H. the Duke of Connaught from Hartham Park to Chippenham. 1899

H.M. the Queen, having been pleased to signify her intention of visiting Bristol in November, and of opening the Convalescent Home that had been erected in that city, arrangements were made for the Yeomanry Cavalry of Wiltshire, Gloucester, and Somerset to take part in the Royal Procession through the streets. A squadron, representing the several troops, was accordingly detailed to proceed to Bristol on the 15th November.

The squadron, which was commanded by Major the Marquis of Bath, was composed as follows :—

Chippenham: 1 Regtl.-Sergt.-Major, 13 N.C.O.'s and men.
Devizes: 14 N.C.O.'s and men.
Malmesbury: 15 N.C.O.'s and men.
Marlborough: 9 N.C.O.'s and men.
Rood Ashton: 22 N.C.O.'s and men.
Salisbury: 6 N.C.O.'s and men.
Warminster: 1 Sergt.-Major, 11 N.C.O.'s and men.
Swindon: 1 Quartermaster, 1 Sergt.-Major, 10 N.C.O.'s and men.

the other officers being Captain Fuller, Lieutenants Sir T. Fowler, G. Mackay, H. Spencer, and 2nd Lieutenant Thornton.

The squadron left in three special trains from Marlborough, Salisbury, and Swindon, timed to reach Bristol

1899 by 11 a.m. Stabling was provided for the horses, and lunch in a tent in the Cattle Market for the men.

Her Majesty arrived at Bristol by train at 2 p.m., and was received by a salute of 21 guns fired from Durdham Down.

The Queen entered her carriage and drove in procession through the city to the Convalescent Home. The Royal Wilts, the Gloucester, and North Somerset Yeomanry Cavalry formed the escort to the carriages with a squadron of Life Guards, the Gloucester Hussars escorting the first five carriages, while the Royal Wilts, the North Somersets, and the Life Guards were in immediate attendance on Her Majesty.

On arriving at the City Council House the procession halted, and an address of welcome was presented by the Lord Mayor, to which the Queen made a gracious reply. The Lord Mayor, Mr. Herbert Ashman, then received the honour of knighthood, and the procession resumed its progress to the Home, passing on the way a remarkable body of 27,000 school children, who sang the National Anthem as Her Majesty passed. The ceremony of opening the Home having been duly performed, the Queen returned to the station by another route, and left for London at 4 p.m.

Upwards of 8,000 men of the various arms of the service were on duty in the City during Her Majesty's visit, among them being the two battalions of the Wiltshire Volunteers to the number of 1,000 officers and rank and file.

The entire ceremony was got through without a hitch of any kind, and the Queen was pleased to send a telegram on her arrival in London, expressing her satisfaction.

The visit of the squadron to Bristol was most satisfactory in every respect. On the 23rd November, Colonel Long issued the following order :—

"The O. C. desires to express his great satisfaction with the turn- 1899
out of the squadron at Bristol.

"The general appearance of the men left nothing to be desired, and the horses were excellent; he heartily congratulates the regiment upon having had the honour to take part in the proceedings attendant on the visit of H.M. the Queen to the West of England."

On the 24th November the G. O. C. Southern District issued an order as follows:—

"The G. O. C. has much pleasure in acceding to the request of the Lord Mayor of Bristol to convey to the officers, N.C.O.'s and men of the Regular and Auxiliary Forces present during the visit of H.M. the Queen to Bristol on the 15th November, the thanks of the Lord Mayor and the Royal Reception Committee for the great assistance of the troops towards making the day's ceremony such a success."

Meanwhile the difficulty with the Transvaal Republic was rapidly coming to a crisis. The protest made by Mr. Chamberlain against the dynamite monopoly was made in January, and immediately afterwards a meeting was held by the Johannesburg mining community to protest against the methods of the Boer government. The question had now been more or less narrowed down to a discussion of the terms on which the English settlers might acquire the franchise, Mr. Chamberlain being of opinion that if they once obtained a proper representation in the Boer parliament, matters would right themselves in course of time.

Mr. Kruger's government, after first repudiating Mr. Chamberlain's right to interfere at all, eventually consented to a conference at Bloemfontein. There Sir Alfred Milner, as representative of the British Government, met Mr. Kruger and Mr. Steyn. The conference lasted from the 31st May to the 5th June. Several evasive and futile propositions were made by the Transvaal government, but were so manifestly contrived to leave the so-called "Uitlanders" without any real representation that they were

1899 rejected by Sir A. Milner, and the conference broke up without coming to any agreement.

Further proposals were made of a similar character by the Transvaal government, and the negotiations were continued at Pretoria until the end of August. Meanwhile there had been a debate on the 28th July in the British parliament, and the tone of the speeches of the Opposition leaders had the unfortunate effect of encouraging Mr. Kruger to remain as obstinate as ever, until finally, at the end of September, notwithstanding the urgent advice of his well-wishers in the Cape Colony, he abruptly revoked all his former offers, and flatly refused to continue the discussion.

The progress of these protracted negotiations had been anxiously watched in the Colonies. On July 11th an offer to provide volunteers for the war, which now sooner or later seemed inevitable, had been made by Queensland, and this example was speedily followed by the other Australian Colonies and by Canada. The British government, anxious as it was to avoid war, could not be blind to the threatening aspect that the quarrel had now assumed, nor to the fact that the military strength of the Cape and Natal was dangerously weak, there being less than 12,000 men available to defend the two Colonies. At a Cabinet Council on the 8th September, it was decided to send 10,000 more men there, of which 6,000 were to sail at once from India for Durban. President Kruger now demanded explanations as to the movements of troops, and the government made a last effort to preserve peace by proposing another conference. This Mr. Kruger refused to consider, and in consequence received a warning that he was pushing his resistance to a dangerous point.

Several military precautionary measures were now ordered. The Lancashire Regiment was sent to occupy

the Orange River Bridge and the town of Kimberley; 1899
Colonel Baden-Powell, with 700 men, was sent to Mafeking; and General Penn-Symons, with the troops in Natal to the number of 4,000, was ordered to Dundee.

But Mr. Kruger had now made up his mind to fight, and to commence to fight before the troops from India should arrive. For months past arms and ammunition had been poured into the Transvaal by the Delagoa Bay railway, his burghers had received their orders, and his plan of campaign was decided on. He, therefore, on the 25th September, despatched an "ultimatum" to the British government. This contained four demands—

1. That the differences between the two countries should be submitted to arbitration, the Transvaal being treated as an entirely independent State.

2. That the British troops should be withdrawn from the frontiers.

3. That all troops landed since the 1st June should be withdrawn from South Africa.

4. That the troops then on the seas should not be landed.

Notwithstanding the amazing insolence of this demand, Sir Alfred Milner made a last attempt to effect a peaceable agreement. But it was too late; on the 2nd October the Boer commandoes were called out, and the old battle ground of Laing's Nek, on the Natal border, was occupied by an army of 10,000 men under General Joubert.

The fact was that Mr. Kruger and the Boer governments, both of the Transvaal and the Free State, were convinced that the British government, egged on by Mr. Rhodes and the Rand magnates, were really meditating an attack on the independence of the two Republics, and was only waiting for a good excuse and a favourable opportunity.

1899 They had been thoroughly and justifiably alarmed by the Jamieson Raid, an unhappy enterprise, whose conception was as iniquitous as its military conduct was imbecile. From that moment the Boers were convinced of the necessity of being prepared for the attack of the stronger power that they imagined lay behind the authors of the Raid, and had unceasingly been arming in preparation for the final struggle they deemed inevitable.

The Orange Free State, little as it had to complain of, was easily drawn into the struggle by President Steyn, a restless and ambitious man, tempted by the bait of succeeding Mr. Kruger as President of a united Boer Republic stretching from the Zambesi to the Cape; while Boer emissaries had been for years busy among the Dutch farmers of the Cape Colony, preaching sedition, distributing arms and ammunition, and receiving pledges of support.

The ultimate aim of the two Presidents and the Cape rebels was indeed the same, namely the establishment of a United Republic of South Africa, and the expulsion of the British. But the methods which the two parties intended to pursue differed. Mr. Kruger relied on his Mausers, backed by the armed support of the Cape rebels; the Cape rebels relied on attaining their object by making use of Parliamentary forms, backed by Mr. Kruger's Mausers in reserve.

But the surrender after Majuba was now to bear its fatal and inevitable fruit. President Kruger was convinced that a few successes at the commencement of the war, combined with a resolute attitude, would bring any British government to its knees; he judged the time favourable for action, as indeed it was; and he declared war, confident that the Cape Dutch would rise at once in his support, and confident, too, that his commandoes would be in full occupation of Natal, and in possession of the coveted port of Durban long before fresh troops from either India or England could be landed. 1899

Fortunately, the want of organization and supplies delayed the army under Joubert, while, thanks to the admirable arrangements of the Indian government, the Indian contingent landed at Durban on the 8th October, a full week before it had been expected. The fresh troops were at once hurried up to Ladysmith by rail, and the intended Boer advance into Natal was for the time checked.

The war commenced with a few delusive successes for the British arms, and the country indulged in vain hopes of an early and victorious termination of the war.

But the hard-won fights at Dundee, Talana, and Elandslaagte only resulted in the shutting up of Sir G. White and his army in Ladysmith; while in the west, Lord Methuen, after his victories at Belmont and Modder, was brought to a standstill in front of the impregnable position of Magersfontein.

Thus the end of the year found Kimberley, Mafeking, and Ladysmith closely invested by the enemy, the army that was to have invaded the Transvaal from the Cape Colony halted in front of Colenso, and the utterly inadequate force under General French the only obstacle to a victorious march to Cape Town.

Well, indeed, it was for us that Mr. Kruger's hatred of Natal, and his wild desire to obtain the port of Durban, kept his best troops at Ladysmith, on the east, while the bait of Mr. Rhodes' presence at Kimberley, and the desire of inflicting a blow on the hated Rhodesians by the capture of Mafeking, paralysed his forces on the west.

For 10,000 resolute men could have easily brushed aside General French's small command, able commander as he was; the Cape farmers would have been forced to abide

1899 by their promises and to rise whether they liked it or not; and acting as this army would have done, on interior lines, there would have been literally nothing whatever to prevent an unopposed and triumphal march to the very walls of the castle itself.

The commencement of the war by their determined adversary had found the British government vacillating and irresolute; anxious to preserve peace; unwilling to begin warlike preparations, even when peace seemed beyond hope, for fear of precipitating a war. It found the British Opposition ready to use any stick to beat the government dog with: ready to complain that the war had been deliberately provoked on the one hand, and on the other that proper preparations had not been made for fear of provoking it. It found the British War Office, of course, utterly unready; not in the least realizing the magnitude of the struggle it was to embark in; and, in spite of the repeated warnings of its own intelligence department, as usual, intent only on doing things "on the cheap", and refusing to countenance anything that cost money; a misjudged parsimony that had its natural sequence in the appalling waste and profligate lavishness that characterized the later phases of the war.

The result was that the situation at the end of the year found the War Office at its wit's end to provide the necessary reinforcements, and particularly the mounted troops, that every General in South Africa was clamouring for.

It was at this juncture that the Marquis of Lansdowne conceived the brilliant idea of calling on the Yeomanry Cavalry to meet, at least, the last deficiency. Now it had happened that Colonel W. H. Long, at the Warminster cattle show, had made, on the 14th December, before the question of employing the Yeomanry in the field had been

mooted at all, a remarkable and almost prophetic speech 1899
as to the duty of the county to support the Yeomanry Cavalry. Whether this speech suggested the idea to Lord Lansdowne or not, at any rate the county of Wiltshire has the honour of owning both the man who conceived it and the man who was the first to carry it into execution.

A few days after Colonel Long's speech, Lord Lansdowne called a meeting together at the War Office of some Yeomanry commanding officers, Lords Chesham, Harris, Valentia, Colonel Long, and one or two others being present. Lord Lansdowne invited these officers to consider whether it would be possible to provide from their regiments a limited number of mounted men, to the number of three or four thousand, for service in South Africa.

This proposition having been received with the greatest enthusiasm by all present, on the 20th December an order was issued by the War Office calling for volunteers for the new force, and the following day a committee, henceforward known as the Imperial Yeomanry Committee, was formed. To this patriotic body, which consisted of the commanding officers of the principal regiments of the Southern Counties, was entrusted the entire work of the organization and embarkation of the Imperial Yeomanry.

The order of the 20th December, after announcing that the government had decided to raise a mounted infantry force for service in South Africa, as well as to accept the service of a limited number of volunteers, referred to the Yeomanry as follows :—

I. Yeomanry.

1. Her Majesty's Government have decided to raise for active service in South Africa a mounted infantry force, to be named "The Imperial Yeomanry".

2 The force will be recruited from the Yeomanry, but Volunteers

1899 and civilians who possess the requisite qualifications will be specially enlisted in the Yeomanry for this purpose.

3. The force will be organized in companies of 115 rank and file; one captain and four subalterns to each company, preferably Yeomanry officers.

4. The term of enlistment for officers and men will be for one year, or not less than the period of the war.

5. Officers and men will bring their own horses, clothing, saddlery, and accoutrements. Arms, ammunition, camp equipment and transport will be provided by the government.

6. The men to be dressed in Norfolk jackets, of woollen material of neutral colour, breeches and gaiters, lace boots, and felt hats. Strict uniformity of pattern will not be insisted on.

7. Pay to be at Cavalry rates, with a capitation grant for horses, clothing, etc.

8. Applications for enrolment should be addressed to colonels commanding Yeomanry regiments, or to general officers commanding districts, to whom instructions will be issued.

9. Qualifications are: Candidates to be from 20 to 35 years of age, and of good character. Volunteers or civilian candidates must satisfy the colonel of the regiment through which they enlist that they are good riders and marksmen, according to the Yeomanry standard.

CHAPTER XXIII.

The Raising of the Wilts Imperial Yeomanry.

The response throughout the country to the appeal of 1899
the War Office was immediate, and the offices of the Imperial Yeomanry Committee in London were besieged by crowds of candidates, while locally every colonel of Yeomanry Cavalry received offers of service from twice at least as many men as could possibly be required.

In this work Wiltshire was, as ever, in the forefront. The decision to employ the Yeomanry was finally arrived at on the 19th December. On the following day Colonel Walter Long applied for the use of the Artillery Barracks at Trowbridge, which were then fortunately vacant. On the 26th, Colonel Long and the regimental staff of the P. W. O. took possession of the barracks, the majority of the regimental officers joining in the course of the next few days. Indeed, so anxious to be of service were some officers, that, being out with the hounds when the telegrams summoning them were received, they rode straight into Trowbridge just as they were, in their hunting kits, to attend the preliminary meeting. Within a week some two hundred men had enlisted, and by the middle of January there were upwards of three hundred men and two hundred and fifty horses present. As the barracks were only built to contain 132 men and 92 horses they were considerably overcrowded; many men had to be billetted out in the town, while a large number were quartered in the military hospital.

Colonel Long's first Order at Trowbridge was issued on the 26th December. It detailed the officers to take charge

1899 of the several departments engaged in the work of organizing the new corps as follows :—

Clothing Department: Captain Palmer.

Commissariat: Captain Sir J. Dickson-Poynder.

Remounts: Captain J. M. Fuller.

Musketry: Lieutenant Thornton.

To be Adjutant: Lieutenant Thornton.

The 2nd Volunteer Battalion supplied the main guard until the Yeomanry were able to take it over.

On the 30th the detail of duties was issued as under:—

Reveillé: 6.45 a.m.

Stables: 7 to 8 a.m., 4 to 5 p.m.

Breakfast: 8 a.m.

Riding School: 9 to 11 a.m., 2 to 3 p.m.

Drill: 9 to 10, 11 to 12 a.m., 2 to 3 p.m.

On the 13th the death of Sir H. Bruce Meux was notified in Orders, an officer whose untimely decease was greatly regretted by his many friends.

On the 15th the two first companies were formed, being numbered 1 and 2 Co.'s of the Imperial Yeomanry, and officers posted as follows, on the 18th :—

To be Section Commanders: Captain Stanley Clarke, Lieutenant Henderson; to command the Gun Section: Lieutenant Smith-Bingham; but the final posting of all the officers was not completed until the 24th February. It will be noted that Wiltshire provided the Regimental Staff of the 1st Regiment Imperial Yeomanry as well as the officers of the three Wilts Companies.

Colonel Long's intention was at first to raise one squadron for active service, but so many applications for enlistment were received that first two, and then three, squadrons were formed.

The first two squadrons raised were posted, as before mentioned, to the 1st Regiment Imperial Yeomanry, and numbered 1 and 2, Nos. 3 and 4 being the Gloucester and Glamorgan Companies. If the composition of the 1st Regiment Imperial Yeomanry had been delayed a short time, the County would probably have found all four companies, as they could without doubt have been easily raised. As it was, this corps being already completed, the third Wiltshire Company had to be posted to another regiment, the 16th Imperial Yeomanry, under the command of Colonel Ridley, late 7th Hussars. 1899

While the enlistment and organization of the three service squadrons was proceeding at Trowbridge, the County at large was eager to help and second Colonel Long.

The Government allowed a sum of £25 per man for clothing and equipment, and £40 per horse, but a public subscription was initiated by Lord Lansdowne to supplement this. Lord Lansdowne headed the list himself with £500, and the total speedily ran up to over £7,000.

A number of the past and present officers joined together to provide a Colt gun for the regiment. These were Colonel Sotheron-Estcourt, Captain G. Palmer, and Messrs. C. N. Phipps, M. Meredith Browne, L. R. Curtis, R. C. C. Long, A. Grant-Meek, R. W. Merriman, G. P. Goldney, J. Blake Maurice, and J. Sadler. Eventually about £1,000 was subscribed by these gentlemen, and two guns, which did good service in several actions, were purchased and equipped.

Nor were the offers of assistance confined merely to subscriptions of money. Mrs. Benett-Stanford, before it was known that a government grant would be given to purchase a horse, offered to provide one free of charge to any yeoman of the Salisbury Troop who had not got one, and her example was followed by Mr. Weekes, of Cleverton, and several others. Indeed, everyone was eager to

1899 contribute something, however small, as far as their means would allow of. Thus the head-gardener at Wilton sent a pair of field-glasses, Mr. Fuller, a saddler, of Urchfont, offered to fit any saddle sent to him without charge, and throughout the county similar generosity was displayed by the local tradesmen.

The County Fund provided many articles of equipment which could not be provided out of the government grant, but which added greatly to the comfort of the men, and in addition paid the premiums required* to insure the life of each yeoman proceeding on service for the sum of £250. These premiums amounted to £3,511. The expenditure out of the government grant for clothing, etc., for the men and officers amounted to £5,542; for saddlery and horse equipment, £6,500; and for the horses themselves, £19,527.

It proved most unfortunate that no arrangements were made to send out all Yeomanry regiments with a full complement of their own horses—animals which had been thoroughly trained and were fit for work. The English horses did far better than those of any other breed in South Africa, and those companies which were fortunate enough to take their own mounts with them had a very great advantage over those which were hurriedly mounted at the base on animals that were not only entirely untrained, but which had only just been landed after voyages of many weeks, and even months, and which were in consequence quite unfit for work of any kind. Indeed, many of these unfortunates could not even be shod on account of the state their feet were in from having stood in muck up to their hocks during the entire voyage. They had to be served out and ridden up country all the same, and were, of course, hopelessly lame after a march or two on the stony ground. This arrangement was also exceedingly

* In the Prudential Life Insurance Company.

hard on many yeomen who had given a great deal more 1899 for their horses out of their own pockets than the government allowance. For, once passed into the ranks, the horses ceased to be private property, and when left behind were taken possession of by the military authorities and served out to other men. In consequence the unfortunate owners of these not only had to content themselves with the very inferior foreign horses served out at the base, but frequently had insult added to injury of the most aggravating description by seeing their own valuable animals ridden by other yeomen who came out after they did. The Wiltshiremen were, however, more fortunate than many other corps, as they did bring out, at any rate, about half of their own horses.

There was, of course, keen competition among the Imperial Yeomanry regiments to obtain early dates for embarkation. As the Royal Wiltshire had been the first in the field the expectation that the 1st Imperial Yeomanry would be the first to embark was only natural, and the drills and other necessary preparations were accordingly hurried on with the greatest energy. The dreadful weather that prevailed during the whole time the troops were at Trowbridge made riding drills in the open air nearly impossible, but this difficulty was met by hiring a large circus tent to form a supplementary riding school.

By the end of January the contingent was practically ready, and was inspected by General Sir Baker Russell, the G. O. C. Southern District, and, as the orders for embarkation were daily expected, on the 1st February the whole contingent was entertained at what was meant to be a farewell dinner by Mr. Hooper-Deacon.

But the pressure on the transport department of the Imperial Yeomanry Committee was very great, as nearly all the available ships had been already chartered by the

1899 War Office for the conveyance of the Regular troops, and some delay was inevitable. It is to be feared, too, that some little favouritism was shown in the matter of the embarkations, regiments "with friends at court" being shipped without reference to their readiness to take the field. At any rate there were many deficiencies among those first landed in Africa; one, for instance, being unprovided even with cloaks, a deficiency that had to be met by the rather savage expedient of issuing an extra horse blanket to each trooper, with a hole cut in it for him to put his head through.

However this may be, the two troopships *Afric* and *Goth*, each of which had been named as reserved for the 1st, sailed with other corps, and it was not until the 25th February that the contingent received its orders to embark.

The 1st and 2nd Companies were ordered to proceed by train to Liverpool on the 27th to embark on the hired transport *Cymric* at the Canada Dock. On the 26th the three companies were paraded for a last inspection by Colonel Long, who handed over the command of Nos. 1 and 2, with the gun section, to Lieut.-Colonel Chaloner. The troops then attended a farewell Divine Service, at which the Rector of Trowbridge, the Rev. A. C. Dudley Ryder, officiated.

The transport arrangements, which were made by Captain Sir J. Dickson-Poynder, were carried out without a hitch, and on Tuesday, the 27th, the two companies left, No. 2 and the gun section at 7.30 p.m., and No. 1 two hours later.

The contingent received an enthusiastic "send off" from the people in Trowbridge, a hundred torch bearers lighted the way to the station, and the band of the Volunteer Regiment played them out.

The troops duly arrived in Liverpool the following

morning and embarked on the *Cymric*, Colonel and Lady 1899
Doreen Long, and many other members of the principal families of Wiltshire, being present to bid them farewell.

The other two companies—No. 3 the Gloucester, and No. 4 the Glamorganshire—also embarked, as well as the whole 11th Regiment, composed of the two Kent companies and the two Middlesex companies, and also the Fife Light Horse, in all numbering 97 officers, two warrant officers, 1,102 rank and file, and 427 horses, the whole being under the command of Colonel Mitford, 11th I.Y.

In the afternoon the *Cymric* sailed for Cape Town in the presence of a very large crowd of enthusiastic spectators.

On the 3rd March the 63rd company left Trowbridge by rail for London, and the same afternoon embarked on the *Cornwall* at the Royal Albert Docks, together with two companies of the 12th Regiment, the Herts and Suffolk, and two Irish companies of the 13th Regiment.

This account of the raising of the three Wiltshire companies may be fittingly closed by the following Order issued by Colonel W. H. Long, on the 27th February :—

"On taking leave of his command, from this date, of the Wiltshire Imperial Yeomanry, the Officer Commanding desires to convey to the officers, non-commissioned officers, and men his warm appreciation of the soldier-like spirit and enthusiastic good-will which have marked the conduct of all ranks of the regiment.

"The County of Wiltshire, whose Yeomanry regiment is the premier regiment of Great Britain, small, comparatively speaking, though it is in population, has had the great honour to furnish three complete companies of Imperial Yeomen, with two galloping guns and a gun detachment for service in South Africa. This work has been successfully performed in the short period of ten weeks. It would have been impossible to provide so large a force from this county had not the officers non-commissioned officers, and, especially, the Regimental Sergeant-Major and Permanent Staff of the regiment, devoted themselves with splendid energy and good-will to the performance of the very heavy duties which have devolved upon them.

1899 "The O. C. hopes that those officers, non-commissioned officers, and men who have not been selected for service in South Africa will find, in the knowledge that to their labours is due the creditable record of their county at this period of our national history, consolation for the disappointment he knows they feel at being unable themselves to proceed to the front.

"The O. C. desires to place on record his hearty approval of the way in which the men of his command have conducted themselves during the time they have been assembled in the barracks at Trowbridge. Not only have no complaints reached him from the inhabitants of the town, but he has constantly been assured, by responsible people in the town, that the conduct of the men has left nothing to be desired.

"Having regard to the fact that the work has been extremely heavy, that a great deal has had to be done in a short time, and that the weather has been extremely bad, it is, indeed, creditable that the conduct should, during that time, have been so admirable.

"The O. C. desires to convey his thanks to the officers, non-commissioned officers, and men, and to express to those who are about to proceed on active service his conviction that they will, in all respects, do their duty to their Queen and country, and prove themselves worthy of the old regiment to which they belong. His earnest hope is that they may return in safety from the campaign in which they are about to engage. He feels sure that the honour of the Wiltshire Yeomanry Regiment is safe in the hands of those whom he has had the great honour to command."

APPENDIX TO CHAPTER XXIII.

THE MUSTER ROLLS OF THE THREE WILTSHIRE COMPANIES OF IMPERIAL YEOMANRY.

REGIMENTAL STAFF 1ST REGIMENT IMPERIAL YEOMANRY.

Lieut.-Colonel R. R. CHALONER, late 3rd Hussars and 2nd Wilts Rifles; invalided home April, 1900.

Lieut. and Adjutant CUSTANCE. Promoted from the ranks Invalided home.

Captain and Quarter-Master Sir John DICKSON-POYNDER, Bart., R. Wilts Y.C. Transferred to the Staff of Lieut.-Gen. Lord Methuen, April, 1900. Resigned February 1901.

THE OFFICERS OF No. 1 COMPANY.

Captain George GRAVES, from Militia, returned to England September 1900, resigned February 1901.

Lieut. Sir Thomas FOWLER, Bart., R. Wilts Y.C. Capt. *vice* Graves resigned. Killed in action at Moolman's Spruit, 20 April 1902.

Lieut. C. S. AWDRY, R. Wilts Y.C., served till the return of the first contingent.

Lieut. A. G. N. HENDERSON. Formerly in the Cape Mounted Rifles. Served till the return of the men of the first contingent.

N.C.O. STAFF OF No. 1. Co.*

Regimental-Sergt.-Major F. R Bartholomew	Yeo.
Regimental-Qr.-Mr.-Sergt. E. Morel	Yeo.

* The Author has used every possible care in compiling this muster roll, having compared the Enlistment Roll, the Base Depôt Rolls, and the list of names given in the local newspapers. The initials and spelling of the names frequently differ in all three, so strict accuracy cannot be guaranteed. The addresses are given where these could be ascertained.

Quarter-Mr.-Sergt A Drayson
Col.-Sergt. A. J. Lyford, Swindon .. .. Yeo.
Sergeant Dobbie, W. H., Lyddington
„ Butler, T. W., Devizes . . Yeo
„ Brown, G. E., Potterne .. . .. Yeo.
„ Harrington, P. (Gun Det) .. .. Vol.
„ Rawlins, D. S., Pewsey .. .. . Yeo.
Farrier-Sergt. Allen, G., Camden Town
Sergt.-Cook Woollard, E., Swindon
Corporal Bendrey, E. E., Swindon . .. .. Yeo.
„ Butler, E., Devizes .. . . Yeo
„ England, G. F., Holt
„ Knapp, C. H., Malmesbury . .. . Yeo.
„ Merrywether, G. G , N. Bradley.
„ Nicholson, F. .. . Vol.
„ Williams, E. .. . . Yeo.
Shoeing-Smith Bendy, R., Frome
„ Urch, A., Nunney

No. 1 COMPANY.

Private Axford, H
„ Andrews, H R , Bristol
„ Allsopp, R., West Lavington.
„ Allsopp, J. P., West Lavington
„ Ashley, E.
„ Avery, H. S., Tottenham.
„ Briggs, T. G., Clapham .. . . Vol.
„ Beak, G. B., Devizes.
„ Batten, J. N., Greenwich . .. Yeo.
„ Buckland, A. J. . .. .. . Vol.
„ Bazley, A. F., Staverton.
„ Butler, W., Rowde.
„ Butland, T S , Paignton.
„ Blencowe, New Brighton .. . .. Vol.
„ Barnes, A., Devizes.
„ Brunker, L., Trowbridge
„ Barnard, T H., Marlborough.
„ Booth, J J., Southport.
„ Burnaby, H. B.
„ Bulmer, A. E. Saltburn (Gun Det.) Vol.
„ Brown, H. A. (T. A.), Warminster.

Private Bowden, C. R. K., Newton Abbott
„ Benfield, J., Middlesborough (Gun. Det.).
„ Cole, H. G., Lyneham Green.
„ Collingbourne, E., Lyneham . . . . Yeo.
„ Coles, T. G., Trowbridge.
„ Carpenter, W., Devizes.
„ Clace, R , Devizes.
„ Cole, G. F., Shalbourne . Yeo.
„ Clarke, C. L., Roehampton.
„ Collins, W., W. Kensington.
„ Collins, R., New Marske (Gun Det.) . . . Vol.
„ Clarke, C. W., New Marske (Gun Det.) . Vol.
„ Cleverley, A J., Bowden Hill
„ Cory, R. V , Lancaster Gate.
„ Cole, W. P., Winchfield
„ Cole, G. W.
„ Collett, C. E., Melksham.
„ Cooper, J. C , Swindon.
„ Clarke, H. A , Newbury.
„ Cox, H. E., Stratton St. Margaret . . Yeo.
„ Dew, J. J., Milton.
„ Davies, B. L. J., Road.
„ Duck, A. E., Marlborough . . . . . Vol.
„ Davis, T. E., Swindon.
„ Dobby, W. E., Gainsborough.
„ Dean, F. R.
„ Eacott, W., Westbury.
„ Flemming, J. . . . . . . Vol
„ Fry, W. H., Marden
„ Franks, F., Hammersmith . . . Yeo.
„ Faircloth, J., Corsham.
„ Freeman, H T., Swindon . . . . Yeo.
„ Farris, T., Coombe Bissett
„ Forster, H. G. . . . . Vol.
„ Francis, A C , Tiverton.
„ Fulton, J., Swindon.
„ *Grist, J. P., Rowde . . . . . Yeo
„ *Getson, W.

---

* Privates Grist and Getson were numbered 1 and 2 in the I. Y.

Private Gordon, L.
„ Goodman, C.* (H.) (P.).
„ George, E. L., Swindon.
„ Gregory, R., Swindon.
„ Garrett, W. E., Trowbridge.
„ Goffe, W., Corsham.
„ Harraway, D , Easton . . . Yeo.
„ Herbert, G., Marske (Gun Det.) . . . Vol.
„ Henderson, G. C., Clifton . . . . . Vol.
„ Hudd, H. R., Trowbridge . . . . . . Yeo.
„ Hay, H., Stamford.
„ Horsell, G. W., Swindon . . . . . . Vol.
„ Hunter, R. A.
„ Iles, R. W., Dauntsey.
„ Johnson, W. H., Devizes . . . . Vol.
„ Johnson, W. J., Devizes.
„ Joy, G., Hillmarton.
„ Jefferies, W. J., Shrivenham . . . . Yeo.
„ Kidman, H , King's Lynn.
„ Lucas, R., Bishop's Cannings.
„ Lefroy, E. E., Hereford.
„ Lawson, J. H.
„ Lloyd, A. P., Boncath.
„ Le Gros, T. A., Frome.
„ Morton, H. J., Exmouth.
„ Mackay, D., Durines, N.B.
„ Massingham, J. T., Marske (Gun Det.) . . Vol.
„ Morris, J., Homington.
„ McLouchin, G. . . . . . . Vol.
„ Newman, A. W., Devizes . . . . . . Vol.
„ Norton, G. H. . . . . . . Vol.
„ Pritchett, E. F.
„ Proffitt, W. C., Hayward's Heath.
„ Pullen, R., Holt . . . . Vol.
„ Passmore, A. D., Swindon . . . . . . Yeo.
„ Phipps, B., Shrivenham . . . . . . Yeo.
„ Ruck, W. J.
„ Read, E. C. C., Mexico.

---

* Initials variously given in different Muster Rolls.

Private Read, O. S. C , Mexico.
„ Rogers, J. E., Keevil . .. . Yeo.
„ Randall, T. A., Swindon . .. .. Yeo.
„ Simpkins, H., Stanton St. Bernard.
„ Savage, F., Swindon.
„ Smith, E., London.
„ Steele, A., Glamorgan.
„ Stow, R., Fernhurst.
„ Smith, T. A., Walthamstow.
„ Smith, H. P., Earlscourt.
„ Symes, A. V., Clifton .. . . Yeo.
„ Shute, J. V., Purton.
„ Scammell, C., Hilperton.
„ Squirl, A. W.
„ Slade, F. .. .. Vol
„ Southerne, S.
„ Speke, H., Ilminster.
„ Slade, E. W. . . .. Vol.
„ Short. J.
„ Sawyer, L. J., Broughton Giffard .. .. Yeo.
„ Sweetman, G., West Ashton .. . .. Yeo.
„ Stevens, G. H., Swindon.
„ Truckle, J.* (H.) (T.), Devizes.
„ Turner, W., Potterne.
„ Trollope, H. W., Bristol .. .. .. Yeo.
„ Tucker, C. H., Upavon.
„ Vines, C. D., Buckland Marsh.
„ Vines, J., Burbage . .. . Yeo.
„ Wheeler, H. C., Bradford . .. .. Yeo.
„ Watts, W. E., Bromham.
„ Ward, W. E * (A.) .. .. Vol.
„ Woods, W. F., Trowbridge .. .. .. Vol.
„ Wroth, C , Collingbourne Ducis .. .. Yeo.
„ Wood, L. C., London.

THE OFFICERS OF No. 2 COMPANY.

Captain Stanley Clarke. Formerly in Militia. Killed in action, 26 August 1900.

---

* Initials vary in different Muster Rolls.

Lieut. Lord **Alexander G Thynne**, R. Wilts Y.C.; transferred to the Staff at Bloomfontein.

Lieut. C. M. **Thornton**, R. Wilts, Y.C., invalided home, August 1900; rejoined at Harrismith, March 1901; returned home with first contingent

Lieut. C. **Speke**, promoted Capt., *vice* Stanley Clarke; returned home with first contingent.

Lieut. J. **Cavendish-Browne**. Transferred from No 3 Co.; appointed Lieut., *vice* Lord A. G. Thynne. Killed in action, 23 October 1900.

Lieut. H. **Speke**, promoted from the ranks 1st Co., *vice* Lieut Cavendish-Browne, killed.

Lieut. **St. John Broderick**. From Egyptian Police; re-transferred to the Egyptian Police, January 1901.

Lieut. H B. **Burnaby**, promoted from ranks to No. 2 from No. 1 Co.; remained with the second Contingent.

Lieut C. O **Clarke**, promoted from ranks to No. 2 from No. 1 Co.; remained with the second Contingent.

N C O.'S AND STAFF OF No. 2 Co.

Col.-Sergt T. Cooper, Warminster.		
Qr.-Mr.-Sergt. W. C. Harry, Hullavington	.	Yeo
Sergeant Ferguson, S. J, Tooting		
„ Hill, W. O., Westminster.		
„ Morrison, D. H., Wallingford.		
„ Wrightson, J. F. H, Downton	..	Vol.
„ Harris, F., Warminster	. .	Yeo.
„ Harvey, C. H., Cardiff.		
Farrier-Sergt. Williamson, W.		
Corporal Alwright, T. J.		
„ Butcher, G, Warminster	.	Yeo.
„ Carey, H., Stratford-sub-Castle.		
„ Dean, W. E., Codford.		
„ Pope, E. H., Horningsham	. .. ..	Yeo.
„ Tanfield, W. F., Chippenham	. .	Vol
Lce.-Cpl. Berry, H., Ludgershall.		
„ Brown, H. A., Upton Scudamore	.. ..	Yeo.
„ Farbrother, C. J, Kingston.		
„ Parrott, A. C., Warminster		Yeo.
„ Thomas, A., Cowbridge.		

Sadler Mattingley, A.
Shoeing-Smith Bamsey, P. R., Warminster.
„ Russ, F .. .. Vol.
Bugler Goodwin, F. G , Reading . . Vol.
Private Andrews, W. P.
„ Axford, T. H. O., Frome.
„ Brown, H. A., Upton Scudamore.
„ Burt, H. G., Wardour .. Vol.
„ Blunt, G. C., Wanstead.
„ Bushell, G. H. T
„ Braddon, W. C., Tiverton.
„ Cox, F. E., Frome.
„ Coombs, J., Salisbury.
„ Coles, E L., Warminster . .. .. Yeo.
„ Chatfield, W H., Salisbury.
„ Cator, W. R , Allington.
„ Carabine, T. J., Warminster . . . Vol.
„ Cox, A., Banbury.
„ Clarke, H. F., Hampstead.
„ Cunningham, J., Balham.
„ Chivers, A. W., Calne.
„ Cousins, R. W., East Molesey .. . Vol.
„ Clarke, G. E.
„ Daniell, A. G., Burton-on-Trent.
„ Davey, F., Bath.
„ Dent, W., Wookey.
„ Daniell, C. W. . . Yeo.
„ Dunlop, W. H. S., Jersey.
„ Danby, W.
„ Eden, F. E., Devizes.
„ Featherstone, J., Trowbridge.
„ Foreman, A., Warminster . . Yeo.
„ Ford, E. H., Semley . . Yeo.
„ Foreman, C. W. ... .. Yeo.
„ Fufford, M. C.
Faulkner, W., Bracknell.
„ Franks, M. T., Battersea.
„ Flowers, A. S
„ Flay, A H., Bristol.
„ Griernon, T., New Brompton.

Private Griffin, A. B., Kingbury.
„ Godwin, R., Salisbury .. . Vol.
„ Gent, M. W. .. .. Vol.
„ Hill, J., London.
„ Hill, E. T., Warminster .. . . Yeo.
„ Hill, H. G., Trowbridge .. . .. Vol.
„ Horlock, L., Highbury.
„ Hake, A. H., Ottery St. Mary .. . . Vol.
„ Harvey, L. E., Ashburton.
„ Hayter, G., Reading.
„ Howe, J. P. B., Wolverhampton.
„ Hillier, H.
„ Hobbs, W., Hopton.
„ Isgar, H., Donhead St. Andrew.
„ Irons, W. H., Essex.
„ Jefferys, C O., Maiden Bradley .. .. Yeo.
„ Jeffreys, J W., Bristol.
„ Jeffery, B. W., East Ilsley .. .. .. Vol.
„ Jones, J., Wolverhampton.
„ King, H., Teffont Magna.
„ Keevil, C. H. C., Cricklewood.
„ King, F. C., Holloway .. .. Vol.
„ Keates, G., Brentford.
„ Locke, A. G., Maiden Bradley . Yeo.
„ Lynn, A., Maidenhead.
„ Lewis, F., Llandilo.
„ Maundrell, W., Wootton Bassett.
„ Moore, E. G., Bemerton.
„ Marden, B. J., Westbury.
„ Mitchell, S. T., Swindon .. .. .. Vol.
„ Mellsome, J. E., Box . . .. Vol.
„ Owen, A., Warminster.
„ Oexle, B. F. O, Leyton.
„ Perrin, C. E.
„ Prince, S. H.
„ Phillips, O. J., Middlesborough.
„ Rugg, T., Upton Lovell .. .. Yeo.
„ Rice, A., Harrow.
„ Roper, J., Hawkhurst.
, Relf, F., Hawkhurst . . . Vol

Private Read, T., Tunbridge Wells.
„ Sutton, A. H.
„ Street, S., Teffont.
„ Shepherd, F., Warminster . . ... Yeo
„ Stevenson, R., Dumfermline.
„ Stevens, G., Damerham . .. Yeo.
„ Sowerbutts, A. H., London.
„ Sparrow, E. H. D.
„ Sloper, V. R., Atworth .. . . Yeo.
„ Stanton, E., London.
„ Strugnell, C. .. . .. Vol.
„ Sparrow, P. J., Marston Meysey.
„ Wilkins, H., Frome .. .. Vol.
„ Williams, R., Frome.
„ Warn, F. T., Tetbury . .. .. Vol.
„ Young, F. W., Broadchalke .. .. .. Vol.

THE OFFICERS OF No. 63 COMPANY.

Captain A. Hume. From the Indian Army; left the Co. at Maitland to take up a civil appointment.

Captain A. C. Perry, promoted Capt. *vice* Hume, from Lieut.; invalided home, March 1901.

Lieut. W. M. Swinburne, promoted from the ranks; took command, *vice* Perry, and returned home in command of the men of the first contingent. Died in England soon after his return.

Lieut. A. H. F. Wadmore, promoted from the ranks. Left the Company at Maitland on transfer to the 74th Co.

Lieut. A. Boyd-Carpenter. Joined the Company at Maitland in April 1900. Transferred to the Highland Light Infantry, December 1900.

Lieut. Vere Cole. Transferred from the D.C.O.S. Wounded and invalided home, June 1900.

N.C.O.'S AND STAFF OF No. 63 Co.

Squadron-Sergt.-Major S. Whiston. Trans. Staff 16th I.Y.
„ „ „ Holliday, pro. *vice* Whiston, died.
„ „ „ J. Robarts, pro. *vice* Holliday, deceased.
Qr-Mr.-Sergt. W. S. Griffiths, pro. Regt.-Qr.-Mr.-Sergt. 16th I.Y.
„ „ T. E. Alexander, pro. *vice* Griffiths.

Sergt. Beirman, late Grenadier Guards
„ Causton, E. C.
„ Jeffreys, W. H.
„ Mayes, —.
„ Pinckney, W
„ Wells, C.
Far -Sergt. Simmonds, —
Sadler Moxham, —
Corpl. Andrews, A
„ Hall, S A. (Vol)
„ Harrison, A
„ Holloway, J. H.
„ March, A. C.
„ Oxley, A S.
„ Peck, A.
„ Ponton, L. (Yeo.)
„ Portch, S. (Yeo.)
„ Swanborne, L.
„ Taylor, E. J.
„ Wakefield, E. H.
Bugler Rayson, S.
Pvte. Allen, G. T.
„ Allard, C. H.
„ Argyle, J. A. H.
„ Alexander, C.
„ Buckland, W. F.
„ Burford, H.
„ Blandford, W. J.
„ Ball, L. P.
„ Beasley, W. E
„ Crocker, G.
„ Cuff, A. J, Frome
„ Cooper, A. (Vol)
„ Cousens, H. S.
„ Cohen, G. M. N. (Vol.)
„ Cripps, G. H.
„ Clark, E. K.
„ Dixon, H.
„ Dean, H.

Pvte. Davis, F. G.
„ Dowell, G. T. (Vol.)
„ Ellis, T. O.
„ Flack, O. S.
„ Freeman, D.
„ Fyfe, J (Vol.)
„ Frost, F. D.
„ Goulter, P. C. (Vol.)
„ Gater, A. H (Yeo.)
„ Grainge, C. R.
„ Howells, A.
„ Howarth, S.
„ Higham, A. H.
„ Hunt, G. E
„ Hewett, H. E. J.
„ Hoe, S. E. A.
„ Ingham, J. H.
„ Jones, E. E. (Vol.)
„ Jarvis, S. E.
„ Jarvis, C S. T
„ King, H. G. (Yeo.)
„ Kent, C. H. (Vol.)
„ King, A.
„ Kidman, G.
„ Ledbury, E
„ Locke, C. H. J.
„ Lugg, S. P
„ Lakin, A.
„ Morris, J.
„ Mathews, P. A., Byfleet
„ Maidment, J.
„ Miles, W. J.
„ Munro, D.
„ Munro, C.
„ Moore, E. L.
„ Marshman, G. C.
„ O'Reilly, G W.
„ Oxley, A. E.
„ Perry, C. S.
„ Pidding, C.

Pvte. Preston, W. L.
„ Peacock, T. E.
„ Read, A. H.
„ Rose, F.
„ Rayson, S.
„ Railton, J. E.
„ Ramsey, A. D.
„ Sweete, W. G.
„ Shoebridge, F.
„ Selfe, S. R.
„ Sutton, W. H. (Vol.)
„ Stone, W. B.
„ Smith, F. C. (Vol.)
„ Smith, W. J.

Pvte. Shee, C. W.
„ Strother, W. L. D.
„ Sutton, C. J.
„ Skingley, A. C C.
„ Smith, A. T.
„ Taberham, W. W.
„ Taylor, F. G. (Vol.)
„ Trinder, G.
„ Whiteside, N., Southport
„ West, A. B. (Vol.)
„ Wilson, R. G.
„ Williams, J.
„ Young, J.

NAMES OF MEN NOT IN BASE ROLLS.*

No.	
119	Bulman, H. G.
150	Booth, C. W.
9,345	Benfield, J.
9,323	Stevens, C. H.
9,318	Stanton, E.
196	Tee, J. G.
9,360	Williams, P. S
	Wise, H. T., Hospital Dresser
11,647	White, W. (Farrier)

---

* These men appear in the Enlistment Roll, but not being on the Base Rolls, it cannot be stated with certainty what Companies they belonged to.

CHAPTER XXIV.

The Campaign against Prinsloo.

1900 After an uneventful voyage, the *Cymric* arrived at Cape Town on the 23rd March. The men and horses were immediately landed, and marched up to the Base Camp of the Imperial Yeomanry at McKenzie's Farm, near Maitland, about five miles out of Cape Town.

The *Cornwall* arrived on the 30th March, and the 63rd Company with the other Yeomanry on board landed and were marched up to the Base Camp.

The deficiency in horses was made good by the issue of the required numbers from those already at the Base Remount Depôt.

Owing to the difficulty of keeping the army under Lord Roberts supplied with food and ammunition by means of a single line of railway upwards of 800 miles in length, great difficulty was at this time experienced in providing railway transport for the troops, and in consequence there were very soon a great number of men accumulated at the Bases in or about Cape Town.

There were at McKenzie's Farm no less than nine regiments of Imperial Yeomanry together at one time, besides 1,500 remounts, and the water supply became exceedingly difficult to manage. The delay was, in a way, useful, as it afforded time for drills and musketry, both of which were much needed by some corps; but the camp had not been intended to provide accommodation for so many men and horses, and notwithstanding the efforts of the Base Staff, it was decidedly lacking in many requirements, and not particularly healthy, the weather being exceedingly hot. There was a good deal of sickness among the officers, and

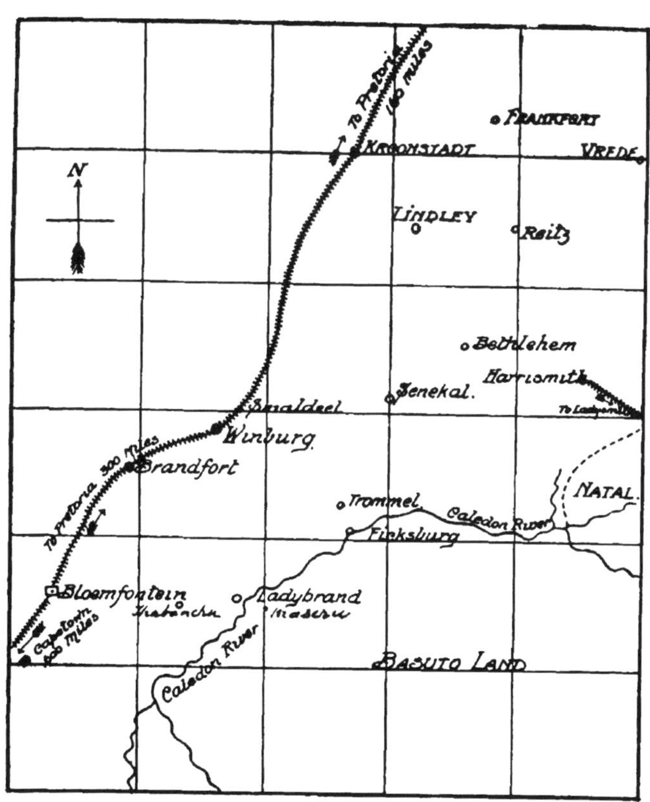

Map to illustrate the campaigns of General Rundle in the Orange Free State, 1900-1901.

This Map is divided into 60-mile squares.

among these was Colonel Chaloner, who, from incautious exposure to the sun, was unfortunate enough to be first sent to hospital and then invalided home. As Colonel Golightly had not yet arrived, the regiment was temporarily commanded by Major Wyndham-Quin. 1900

On the 14th April a parade was held on foot of all the Imperial Yeomanry in camp. Nine regiments, numbering nearly 5,000 officers and men, were present, and made a most imposing spectacle, the line of regimental quarter columns at close interval being over a mile in length, this being the formation in which the troops were in on the parade line previous to marching past the Base Commandant.

On the 16th April the long expected order to move up country arrived, and No. 2 Company left the camp at McKenzie's Farm. It entrained at Cape Town the same day, and arrived on the 19th at Springfontein, a station a few miles across the border of the Orange Free State, where it was encamped.

The following day (the 17th) No. 1 Company, the Gun Section, and the Head-Quarter Staff of the 1st Imperial Yeomanry left Cape Town, and joined No. 2 Company at Springfontein on the 20th.

On the 18th the 3rd and 4th Companies left Cape Town, but instead of proceeding direct to Springfontein they were for some reason detrained at Norvals Pont, the bridge by which the railway crosses the Orange River, at midnight on the 20th; but these companies joined the first two at Edenburg, another station on the railway, to which place they had marched after leaving their tents and stores at Springfontein.

The regiment was at once employed in escorting convoys and various reconnaisances, and during one of the former had its first casualty, on the 28th April, by the unfortunate

1900 death of Private Harris, of the Gloucesters, who was accidentally run over by a waggon and killed.

Eventually the regiment reached Bloemfontein on the 1st May, and after a halt of three hours there, marched to Springfield, and thence by easy marches to Thabanchu, where, on the 4th May, they joined the 8th Division under General Rundle.

General Rundle was now engaged in the preliminary movements by which he intended to try and surround the Boer forces then operating in the Eastern corner of the Free State. His plan was, briefly, to drive them into the Brandwater Basin, a valley on the upper part of the Caledon River, enclosed on the Free State side by a range of mountains, and with Basutoland, into which the Boers dare not venture, to the south, the Caledon River being the dividing line of the two States. The 1st I.Y. was somewhat fortunate in being kept more or less intact during the campaign in the Free State, in that it was attached at least all through to the one, the 8th, Division. Many of the regiments of the I.Y. indeed found themselves split up, even before they landed in Africa. The 16th I.Y., to which the 63rd belonged, for instance, never saw two of its companies, the 50th and 65th, at all, these being landed at Beira for service in Rhodesia, the place of one being taken by the 74th Company belonging to the 17th Regiment, which corps, or at least two of its companies, with the Regimental Staff, had also been sent to Beira.

On the 5th May the 1st Regiment went into action for the first time, the Staff Gun Section, No. 2 and No. 4 Companies being engaged all day in a strong reconnaisance of the enemy's position. The Wiltshires were fortunate enough to escape without a casualty, but the Glamorgans had one man wounded by a shell splinter.

On the 11th May No. 2 Company was posted to General Clements' Brigade, half the Company, under Lieutenant Thornton, being sent to join his column at Winburg, the other half being ordered to Ficksburg, where it remained in garrison for some weeks. 1900

Lieutenant Thornton and his detachment furnished General Clements' advance guard on the march of the column from Winburg to Senekal, there being no other mounted troops with the Brigade.

The 1st Regiment was now employed in various duties with the Division in the neighbourhood of Thabanchu. On the 15th May, Major Wyndham-Quin, with No. 4 Company, occupied Ladybrand, No. 1 being sent to the Leeuw River Mills, about fifteen miles from that place.

On the 24th, the Queen's birthday, the garrison of Ladybrand, which had now been increased by the arrival of a company of the Worcester Regiment, held a parade, at which the Proclamation announcing the annexation of the Free State, henceforward styled officially the Orange River Colony, was read, and on the 26th this event was celebrated with races and athletic sports of various kinds, at which Sir G. Lagden, the British Resident in Basutoland, was present.

On the 25th Senekal, a place that seemed destined to be unlucky to the Imperial Yeomanry, was the scene of the first of several unfortunate affairs. A party of I.Y., under Major Ashton, with which was a detachment of No. 2 Company, rode into the town in order to ascertain if there was a sufficient supply of water there for the Division. Major Ashton received the submission of a Boer, who was represented to be the Landroost of the place. He then posted picquets round the town and proceeded to collect the arms of the inhabitants.

While this was going on, Major Dalbiac, with a

1900 number of the Middlesex Yeomanry, rode in, and there being no sign of the enemy, dismounted in the centre of the town. His men were scarcely off their horses when a hot fire was opened on the place from the surrounding hills.

Major Ashton drew in his picquets and made hasty preparations for a defence, while he endeavoured to destroy as many of the rifles he had collected as he could; but Major Dalbiac, a brave and reckless officer, with a fanatical belief in the power of mounted men, hastily mounted, and, followed by those of his men who happened to be at hand, made a determined charge on a steep hill, occupied by a number of Boers, just outside the town.

The gallant Dalbiac made three efforts to close with the enemy, but fell himself, while most of the men who followed him were either killed or wounded.

The noise of the firing was heard by General Rundle, who sent up some guns, which speedily drove off the enemy. Major Ashton then withdrew his force without loss.

The men of the No. 2 Company captured a Boer flag in this affair, which was brought back to England and presented to Colonel W. H. Long.

On the 30th May news reached General Rundle of the evil plight of the unfortunate 13th I.Y. at Lindley. He was too distant to be able to give them any actual assistance, but hoping to draw off some of the Boer forces and relieve the pressure on them, he attacked the enemy about twelve miles from Senekal.

The Boers were very strongly posted, and the attack, which failed to dislodge them, and indeed was never seriously pressed, ceased in the afternoon, and the troops returned to camp.

This affair, which did nothing at all to assist the 13th,

who surrendered the next day, cost a number of lives, the 1900 Guards' Brigade in particular suffering very severely. The Wiltshire Companies of I.Y. were not engaged in the action.

On the 31st General Clements joined the 8th Division at Senekal, and marched with it to Ficksburg, where Lieutenant Thornton rejoined the other half of the 2nd Company, and the same day Colonel Golightly arrived and took over the command of the 1st Regiment from Major Wyndham-Quin. From this date until the 25th July the 1st I.Y. was employed in escort duty and reconnaissances with the 8th Division, being daily under fire, for the whole country was alive with scattered bands of the enemy.

Meanwhile the 63rd Company had been undergoing a weary delay at the Base, owing to the impossibility of providing transport by rail; but at last it was, with the 66th Company, allowed to march to Stellenbosch.

On the 28th the 63rd was moved by rail to Colesburg, and on June the 6th to Winburg, in the Free State, where some days after it was joined by the 66th Company, and with it posted to the Brigade commanded by General Clements.

By the middle of June the preparations for a campaign against the Boer forces in the Orange River Colony were completed, and the operations, in which all the three Wiltshire companies took an active part, commenced. The three Boer Generals, De Wet, Prinsloo, and Olivier, with about 10,000 men, well supplied with artillery, were located in the mountainous and difficult country in the neighbourhood of Bethlehem, and it was General Rundle's intention to gradually surround them and drive them into a sort of horseshoe, the base of which would be formed by the Caledon River and Basutoland.

The British dispositions were as follows:—

1900 1. At Lindley was General Paget with the 20th Brigade.

2. At Heilbron Generals Macdonald, Hunter, Bruce-Hamilton, and Broadwood, with two Infantry Brigades, a Brigade of Regular Cavalry, Lovat's Scouts, the 12th I.Y., and two companies of the Scottish I.Y. This force had been concentrating at Frankfort since June 2nd.

3. At Winburg, General Clements, with the 6th, 62nd, 63rd, and 66th Companies I.Y., and Brabant's Horse, was ordered to march to Lindley by way of Senekal, and to effect a junction there with General Paget.

4. General Rundle himself, with the 8th Division, including the 1st I.Y., occupied a line of country about forty miles in frontage, extending from Ficksburg to Senekal.

On the 18th June the Boers threatened Ficksburg, but the attack came to nothing. Another small action took place the same day at Dornkop, and fighting continued daily at various points while the 8th Division was gradually closing in upon the enemy's left; but the opening of the campaign proper was perforce delayed until General Clements should be ready to act.

On the 21st June the 63rd and 66th Companies were sent with a convoy from Winburg to Senekal, and met General Clements, who was coming into Winburg. The companies remained with his brigade, and early in the morning the next day came under fire for the first time. The troops had hardly left camp when the Boer guns opened fire, but the two companies at once galloped out to the right flank of the enemy, and having dismounted soon obliged them to retire, and the column marched into Winburg without further opposition.

On the 25th June General Clements left Winburg with a very large convoy of supplies, the collection of which had

been the cause of his long delay. The same night the 1900
63rd came under fire for the second time. The force under the command of Colonel Grenfell, composed of the I.Y., Brabant's Horse, and two guns, was detached to capture a Boer camp at Rietspruit. Owing to the treachery of the guide, the place was not reached till after daybreak, and Colonel Grenfell found the enemy in position and ready to receive him.

As soon as it was light enough to see clearly, the Boers opened fire on the column with two guns and two pompons, stampeding many of the horses and causing great confusion, which was increased by a hot rifle fire and the shells from a heavy gun posted on a hill commanding the right flank.

The British guns were brought up, and though many gunners fell, their rapid and accurate practice soon began to tell, and the enemy's fire slackened. At 11.30 a.m. the reinforcements despatched by General Clements, when he heard the heavy firing, made their appearance, and the Boers hastily retired. The British loss in this affair was three killed and twenty wounded. After the action General Clements resumed his march, and arrived at Senekal on the 27th June.

The first move in the campaign was to be the occupation of Bethlehem. The execution of this part of the plan was entrusted to Generals Clement and Paget.

On the 28th General Clements left Senekal. He was at once attacked while on the march by a strong force of the enemy, probably the same commando that had been encountered at Rietspruit, as it had with it the same number of guns and pompons. A running fight was kept up all day, though the Boers avoided coming to close quarters, and the camp was shelled all night, the Veldt being set on fire by the burst of the shells.

1900 The next day the march was resumed under similar conditions. The enemy showed in some force at Zandsspruit, but were easily dislodged, and on the 30th the column reached Kruisfontein, fourteen miles from Lindley.

The next day a patrol of Mounted Infantry and I.Y., pushing on close to Lindley, were suddenly attacked by a Boer Commando while watering their horses.

Two officers, Major Jenkinson and Captain Seely, with several men, were taken prisoners; but the enemy were eventually driven off with some loss, though they succeeded in carrying off their prisoners, and the same afternoon General Clements entered Lindley and joined General Paget.

The following day (2nd July) Generals Clements and Paget marched out with their united forces for Bethlehem, the two columns moving by separate roads, about ten miles apart.

On the 3rd the Boers were discovered in force, occupying a strong position on a rocky ridge across the roads to Bethlehem, and were at once attacked by both columns.

The 63rd and 66th Companies I.Y. advanced in extended order up the slope of the hills occupied by the enemy to draw their fire, this being the usual method of employing the Yeomanry at the commencement of an action. The Boers in this instance reserved their fire until the Yeomen were well within rifle shot, and then opened on them with artillery, pom-poms and rifles. Fortunately the shooting was very indifferent; the British artillery at once came into action, and the Yeomen affected a hasty retreat. The 63rd escaped without any casualties, but the 66th lost one officer and two men. The accurate fire of the artillery eventually dislodged the Boers without the necessity of employing the infantry, but not before the gunners had suffered rather severely by a counter attack from a number

of the enemy who, taking advantage of the broken and 1900
rock-strewn ground, had contrived to creep unseen to within 700 yards of the guns.

These Boers were eventually driven off by a spirited charge of the Australian Bushmen, supported by the C.I.V. guns, but the gunners, who stuck manfully to their posts, lost sixteen men killed and wounded. The Bushmen and I.Y. loss in this action amounted to another sixteen. The enemy here met with turned out to be a rear-guard, with five guns and some pom-poms, covering a very large convoy, and was closely followed up by General Clements until sunset.

The two columns resumed their march, and on the 5th July re-united about four miles from Bethlehem, when Clements sent in a flag of truce demanding the surrender of the town, but received a curt refusal from De Wet, who was in command.

The town of Bethlehem, which for some time had been the headquarters of the Boer forces in the Free State, lies in a deep valley between steep and high hills, the horns of which extended on either flank towards the British position. These hills were occupied by a force of about 4,000 Boers, with six or seven guns of large calibre. The united columns of Clements and Paget amounted to 6,000 men and sixteen guns, so a sharp combat was expected, owing to the difficulties presented by the ground, which was very favourable to the defence, and the superior weight of the Boer guns.

On the 6th the enemy began the action at daybreak by shelling the British camp with a heavy Creusot gun, and the army hastily turned out and deployed for the attack.

General Paget had the right attack, General Clements the left, the I.Y. and Brabant's Horse being on the

1900 extreme left flank. An attempt was made to turn both flanks with the mounted men, but they were too extensive and too strongly held. The position was then shelled until the evening, when the Yorkshire and Munster Regiments were ordered to advance to the attack of the ridge of hill on the Boer left, which they carried by a determined bayonet charge. Night then fell, and orders were issued to hold the position gained, and for a general advance the next day.

Soon after daybreak the action was renewed by an advance of the whole line, covered by artillery fire. The attack was completely successful, the Royal Irish particularly distinguishing themselves by capturing a gun by a fine bayonet charge, the Boers fled in confusion, and the town surrendered.

The British lost 100 killed and wounded in this spirited little combat, of whom about half were Royal Irish. The Wiltshire Regiment (62nd) took part in this action, being in support of the Royal Irish, and lost seven men.

The Boers had apparently made this stand to cover the removal of their stores from Bethlehem, for little was left there out of the large quantity of munitions that were known to have been in the place, except several loads of flour. This, however, was a welcome addition to the scanty rations of the British army, particularly to General Paget's men, who had been on very short allowance for some time.

The following day being Sunday, the troops enjoyed a well-earned rest in the town, and in the afternoon General Hunter's Division marched in.

This account of the march of General Clements' column gives a very fair picture of the life of the British soldier in South Africa.

It was the African winter, and though frost is rare in

the day time, the nights were bitterly cold, the men's water bottles being nothing but a solid mass of ice in the mornings. There was none of the pomp and glory of war, none of the stirring excitement of a pitched battle and the glorious exaltation brought by a decisive victory. The troops plodded on, through icy winds, dust and rain, snow and hail; ill-clothed, fed on the coarsest food, and not too much of that; sleeping on the ground with no covering but a ragged blanket; under fire night and day from an unseen and elusive enemy, and bearing all with a cheerful and dogged endurance beyond all praise. 1900

Surely England owes a debt of gratitude to her gallant sons in the Yeomanry, who, for the most part, accustomed to a life of easy plenty, cheerfully underwent not only the dangers of war, but what is infinitely more trying, the hardships and exposure inevitable to this campaign, animated only by a sense of patriotic duty.

While these operations were in progress, General Rundle on his side had been gradually closing in and shortening the line he was holding with the 8th Division.

All June the 1st I.Y. had been employed in various duties with the Division, the four companies being occasionally together, but more often working independently. They had moved backwards and forwards escorting convoys and artillery to and from Ficksburg, Hammonia, Senekal, and Ladybrand. On the 14th the 2nd Company lost Private Oxle, who was taken prisoner, and on the 1st July No. 3 lost a man in the same manner. The first three weeks in July passed in the same way, and on the 27th the four companies and the guns joined the Division at Commando Nek, losing Corporal Nicholson of the gun section on the march, he being unfortunately drowned when crossing a river.

On the 11th July the 8th Division had joined hands

1900 with General Clements, thus tightening and completing the cordon, and the enemy began to realize the danger of their position.

They were in a difficult and mountainous country, enclosed by a semi-circle of troops rapidly closing in upon them, with the impassable frontier of Basutoland behind them. On the 10th July they released upwards of 700 prisoners, mostly men of the Derbyshire Militia captured at Roodeval, and their main body retired towards the south-east corner of the State.

The Boers now lay concealed in an intricate mass of mountains, the only town remaining in their possession was Fouriesburg, in the Brandwater Basin. The ground they occupied formed a sort of vast horseshoe, the curved end to the north, and the base formed by the Caledon River, across which was Basutoland. Their only exits were by seven well marked Passes, namely, Commando Nek on the south, close to the Basuto Border, Wit Nek on the north-west, Slabbert's Nek and Retief's Nek on the north, and Slaap Krantz on the east, leading into the valley of the Little Caledon, from which last there were two Neks or Passes, Naauwpoort Nek and Golden Gate, facing north-east. All these Passes were watched by Generals Rundle, Campbell, Hunter and Macdonald. General Paget, who had been delayed by want of supplies near Bethlehem, now moved to Slabberts Nek, which he reached on the 20th, and joined hands with General Clements, who was then near Bulfontein. But this delay had the most disastrous consequences, for on the 16th De Wet and Steyn, with 2,000 men and five guns, stole away through Slabbert's Nek, and though hotly pursued by Broadwood, made good their escape with but trifling loss.

Indeed, had the whole Boer army listened to De Wet's

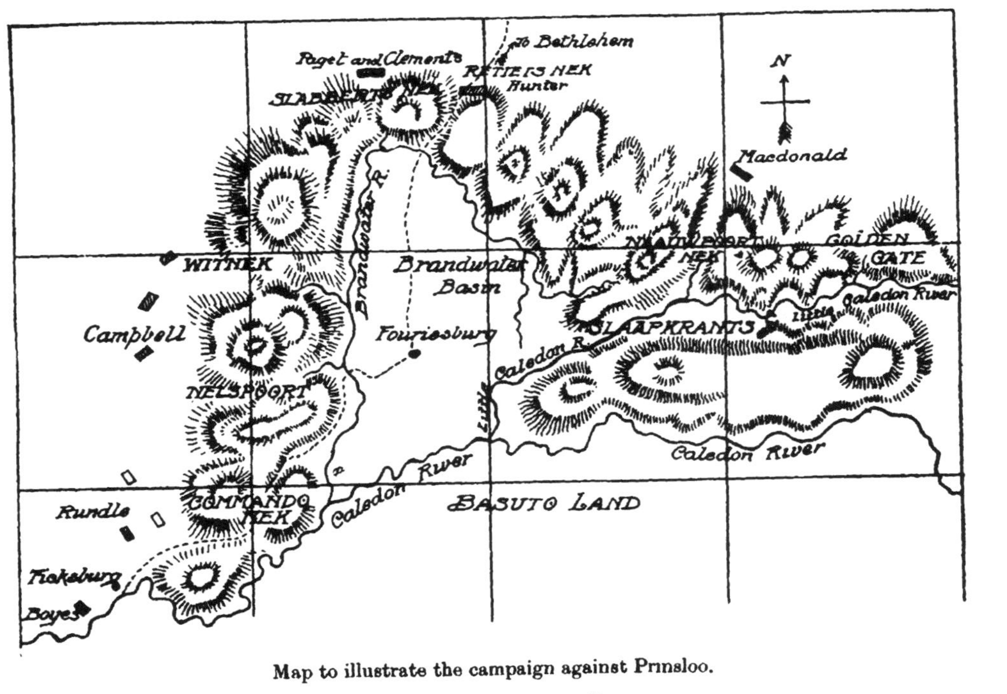

Map to illustrate the campaign against Prinsloo.

This Map is divided into 30-mile squares.

advice, it might possibly have slipped through the cordon 1900
with him; but there was much dissension among the generals; no common plan of action could be arrived at, and finally De Wet went off with his own commando by himself.

On the 23rd July a general forward movement was made; Rundle moved to Commando Nek, Paget and Clements to Slabbert's Nek, and Hunter to Retief's Nek.

On the 23rd the attack was pressed on all sides. Paget and Clements assaulted the pass at Slabbert's Nek, the 63rd Company and the rest of the I.Y. advancing against the centre, while the Royal Irish and Munster Regiments tried to scale the heights on the right and left respectively. But the rocks were so steep, and the Boers so well covered, that but little progress could be made during that day. The attack was renewed the next morning, when it was found that the enemy had evacuated the position during the night.

The troops then moved on through the Pass into the Brandwater Basin, where they found General Hunter, who had stormed Retief's Nek the preceding day, after a rather severe combat, with the loss of twelve killed and seventy-four wounded. Lovat's Scouts particularly distinguished themselves in this action.

The combined force now menaced the Boer positions at Commando Nek, while Naauwpoort Nek was seized after a trifling resistance. But the Pass at Golden Gate had been by some mischance overlooked, and though the omission was observed and a brigade sent off to occupy it, it arrived too late; for Olivier, with the Harrismith Commando, had already slipped through and made good his escape with 1,500 men and five guns.

General Rundle now moved to Fouriesburg and thence to Slaap Krantz, the last of the Boer positions. There

1900 were now between five and six thousand Boers left, with fifteen guns, General Prinsloo being in command.

On the 29th July Slaap Krantz was attacked. This proved a very formidable position, the Pass being steep and narrow, and flanked by precipitous cliffs, so steep as to be nearly impassable. It was held, too, by a strong Boer rear guard, all stubborn and determined men, to the number of 800, with two guns. The action began by a bombardment by the artillery, which lasted all day, and in the morning the troops took up their position for the final assault.

Colonel Golightly with No. 4 Company formed the flanking party of the attack. The Colt guns had been in action all day in the first line, commanded first by Sergeant Harrington and then by Lieutenant Robertson, who, though wounded, returned to his guns as soon as his wound had been dressed. Sergeant Harrington and Private Dean, of the gun section, were also wounded. At midnight the attack was delivered, but the enemy, alarmed by a report of the British being in their rear, and somewhat demoralized by the heavy artillery fire, made but a half-hearted stand, and the Pass was taken with the loss of only ten men. A few prisoners were captured, but the majority rode away into the Little Caledon Valley, hoping to escape by Naauwpoort Nek. Here, however, they were met by Macdonald and the Highlanders, and they returned in an aimless way towards Slaap Krantz, joining Roux's Commando near that place. On the 31st Roux surrendered with 1,200 men.

Prinsloo, finding himself surrounded and outnumbered, entered into negotiations with General Rundle, and on the 4th August surrendered unconditionally with 4,120 men and three guns, the rest of his artillery having been probably concealed or buried in the mountains. In addition,

a very large quantity of ammunition was captured and 1900
destroyed, and an enormous train of oxen and waggons, laden with stores of all sorts, was seized in the Brandwater Basin, together with many thousand head of cattle.

On the whole, therefore, these well-planned and ably-executed operations resulted in success, and for a time it looked as if the enemy's opposition in the Free State had been completely broken.

At the close of the campaign against Prinsloo half the 1st Company was at Leuw River Mills and half with Colonel White at Thabanchu, No. 2 at Ladybrand, No. 3 at Ficksburg, No. 4 at Slaapkrantz, and the 63rd at Retief's Nek. At the end of the month No. 2 relieved No. 3 at Ficksburg, and the half company at Leuw River marched to Ladybrand, leaving a detachment at the former place, which is about fifteen miles from Ladybrand.

The 63rd Company, after Prinsloo's surrender, joined the brigade under General Paget, and escorted the prisoners into Winburg. The country was still full of scattered parties of the enemy, and the rear-guard was occasionally fired on during the march. On arriving at Winburg the prisoners were put on the train and sent down to Capetown, after which the 63rd went back to Senekal in charge of a convoy and 500 horses and mules. After handing these over, the Company returned to Winburg and marched thence to Smaldeel, where they entrained for Pretoria.

On the 8th August the 8th Division, including Nos. 3 and 4 Companies, marched to Harrismith in order to re-open railway communications with Natal.

CHAPTER XXV.

No. 1 and No. 2 Companies.

1900 After Prinsloo's surrender it had been fondly imagined that the war was over, as far, at any rate, as the Free State, now officially annexed under the title of the Orange River Colony, was concerned; but this pleasing delusion was of very short duration.

De Wet, with his commando, was at large in the neighbourhood of Kroonstadt, in the north, and on the 8th August Olivier was reported to be at Frankfort, in the north-east, and marching to join him. Both these commandos very soon showed that they still had plenty of fight left in them, and it became evident that a fresh combined movement would have to be undertaken if the State was to be cleared of the enemy.

General Hunter now moved from Bethlehem to Heilbron, and thence to Lindley, where he arrived on the 11th August. He then sent his sick and wounded, with the animals and waggons captured in the Brandwater Basin, to Kroonstadt, and, relieved of this encumbrance, followed hard on the track of the Boer commandos with his column. He crossed the Rhenoster River on the 13th August, and the next day found Olivier with 1,800 men and six guns posted in a strong position across the road. General Hunter at once attacked the enemy, and after six hours fighting the Boers retired towards Winburg. General Hunter then returned to Heilbron, having lost four killed and 41 wounded in this action, which, though successful in so far that the Boer position was taken, led to no useful result. The enemy's loss was not known.

On the 20th August a detachment of No. 2 Company, under Lieutenant Speke, had a rather nasty experience near Senekal. The party, 15 in number, had been sent from Ficksburg to try and round up some stragglers from Olivier's commando, and, hearing that a number of the Boers were at a farm near Senekal, an attempt was made to surround the place and take them prisoners. The enemy, however, who were much more numerous than was supposed, made such a good defence that they beat off the Yeomanry, who left two killed, Privates T. Brown and Young, and four wounded on the ground. One of the latter, Private Flower, whose wound was not very severe, very pluckily remained with the others and attended to their injuries as well as he could, pretending to the Boers that he was a doctor. The enemy soon afterwards rode off, and the wounded men were recovered and brought in. 1900

On the 24th the 2nd Company was again in trouble. Captain Clarke and Lieutenant Barclay went out with a small force of 200 men, chiefly Leicester I. Y. and Port Elizabeth Guards, under command of Captain Harrison, of the Leicester I. Y., into the Brandwater Basin. Captain Clarke was sent to try and surprise a party of Boers reported to be at a farm in the mountains, and at day-break he surrounded the place with his detachment. Some of the Boers having taken refuge in a cave, Captain Clarke and Lieutenant Barclay attempted to enter it, with the result that the former was killed and the latter severely wounded. Captain Harrison, hearing the firing, came up with the Leicesters, but in the confusion caused by the fall of the two officers, the Boers got away with the loss of one killed and 17 prisoners. Private J. Hill was also wounded.

At this date the British troops occupied Harrismith, Bethlehem, Fouriesburg, and Heilbron, and the railway from Harrismith to Natal was open, but the line from

1900 Naauwpoort through Bloemfontein and Winburg to the Transvaal border was very weakly held.

The author was at Bloemfontein at the time, and remembers well the uneasiness felt there when Olivier's commando was said to be in the neighbourhood of the town. The place itself was quite indefensible, and garrisoned only by two weak companies of I. Y. and four companies of infantry.

It was true that the town was little more than a vast hospital, but the moral effect of the recapture of the capital of the old Free State would have been great, and the interruption of the communications by rail, these would have been extremely inconvenient, to say the least. Kroonstadt, too, which was full of stores intended for the army in the Transvaal, had a garrison of barely 600 men. Fortunately, De Wet seems to have been unaware of this, for he marched all round the place till he struck the railway, which he broke up in several places, and, indeed, very nearly had the luck to catch Lord Kitchener himself, who was then on the line.

Olivier himself, with his commando, was in the neighbourhood of Winburg, where Colonel Ridley, the Lieut.-Colonel commanding the 16th Regiment I. Y., was in command of the garrison, which consisted of 1,600 men, of whom 300 were mounted, and four guns.

On the 20th August Colonel Ridley received orders to move out with his mounted troops towards the Doornberg range of hills, and to join a small column under Colonel Sitwell that was operating in that district. Olivier, having received intelligence of this, promptly attacked him with his whole commando.

Colonel Ridley retired to a farm called Helpmakaar, about ten miles from Winburg, where he was surrounded by the enemy, and, refusing a summons to surrender, was shelled continuously for 48 hours. Colonel Ridley, who 1900 handled his small force with great skill and gallantry, beat off several determined attacks, and held the place until he was relieved by General Bruce Hamilton, who came by train from Heilbron on the 25th.

Colonel Ridley lost 41 killed and wounded in this affair, 33 of which belonged to the Queenstown Volunteers, who had shown conspicuous coolness and courage throughout, and was highly complimented by Lord Roberts for his defence.

After the relief of Helpmakaar the troops returned to Winburg, where General Bruce-Hamilton made arrangements to return by train to Kroonstadt. This Olivier got wind of by tapping the telegraph wires, and after waiting until he thought General Hamilton's men would have left, he attacked Winburg. But the trains had been delayed, Bruce Hamilton's brigade was still there, and he was beaten off after two hours' fighting with considerable loss. The retreating Boers were followed up by Colonel Ridley and his mounted troops, including the Queenstown Volunteers, and one of these, Sladdin by name, being considerably in advance of the rest, finding that he was surrounded by the Boers, posted himself on a small koppie where he was joined by seven of his comrades. There they captured, one after the other, 24 of the enemy as they rode by, and among them Olivier himself and his three sons. They managed to hold their position, though at one time attacked by upwards of 200 Boers, and eventually brought their prisoners safely into Winburg, a feat and success most remarkable for both coolness and audacity.

By this time the whole country was again alive with scattered bodies of the enemy, but the fortunate capture of Olivier had deprived the commandos of their head; there was no one left able to enforce obedience on the inde-

1900 pendent commandants, and their operations were consequently much less dangerous than if they had been directed by a single general of Olivier's capacity and authority.

The majority of the men of Olivier's commando made off in the direction of Ladybrand, where a considerable quantity of stores had been collected. Ladybrand was held by half of the No. 1 Company under command of Captain Graves, and a weak company of the Worcester Regiment.

Another commando was at Thabanchu, threatening the Bloemfontein water-works. On September 1st a column under Colonel White occupied the water-works, driving the enemy back to Thabanchu, but it was found impossible to send any troops to Ladybrand in time to intercept Olivier's men, now commanded by Haasbrock and Fourrie. Orders were sent to Major White, Royal Marines, who was in command at Ladybrand, to evacuate the place and cross over into Basutoland after destroying what stores he should be unable to remove, and to retire to Ficksburg; but the Caledon River was in flood and unfordable, which circumstance gave that officer a valid excuse for remaining where he was, a course which Sir G. Lagden strongly urged him to follow. Major White then moved his force, which consisted of 41 N.C.O.'s and men of No. 1 Company under command of Captain Graves, with Lieutenants Awdry and Henderson, and 90 men of the Worcesters, to a small fort which had fortunately been constructed some time previously, just outside the town. What stores time permitted the removal of were carried into the fort, and the remainder destroyed. Short as the time was the men indulged in a practical joke for the benefit of the expected Boers by filling the emptied rum casks with water, and 100 provision cases with earth.

A party of 21 Imperial Yeomanry that were at Leeuw

River Mills were withdrawn to Ladybrand, and the 31st 1900
August and 1st September were spent in digging trenches and shelters round the position. On Sunday, September 2, at 5 a.m., the advance guard of the Commando were reported near the town, and the troops retired to the fort, which they had hardly occupied when the main body, numbering 3,000 men with four 12-pounder and two 15-pounder guns and two pompoms, arrived.

A flag of truce was sent into Colonel White with a demand for immediate surrender, to which that officer replied that if they wanted the place they could come and take it.

The enemy at once opened a heavy fire of all arms, which continued till late in the afternoon, when a half-hearted attempt to rush the trenches was made, which was easily repulsed. The fire was continued all Monday, and was so well aimed and closely maintained that no one could leave the trenches for food and water during daylight, and even at sunset only at considerable risk, for the position was cramped, and the rifle fire at close range kept up all night. This day Sergeant-Major Lyford was severely wounded, the lower jaw being carried away by a shell. He was sent into the hospital in the town under a flag of truce, and eventually made a good recovery. The horses and oxen, which had been brought into the lines and concealed, most of them in a cave and the rest in a deep ravine adjoining, were also all killed by shell fire, their position unfortunately having been revealed to the Boer gunners by a prisoner who had escaped, and the wagons and water barrels smashed to pieces. Meanwhile Sir G. Lagden and thousands of Basutos had been watching the progress of the fight from the hills across the river with keen interest, and had been trying to communicate with the besieged by heliograph. But Major White had no signalling apparatus, and was

1900 unable to reply until Corporal Blencowe, a Devizes man, who had acquired a slight knowledge of signalling in the Volunteers, improvised one with a bit of looking glass. A message was then received to say that General Bruce-Hamilton was on his way to relieve them, with 5,000 men and 2 guns. But this message unfortunately was read by the Boers, and, disregarding the objurgations and exhortations of their leaders, who urged them to storm the place at once, they began to slip away in detachments.

On Wednesday morning it was found that the whole Commando had disappeared, having lost 47 men killed and wounded, and fired no less than 382 shells into the place during the seige. The relieving column came in about mid-day, but though some pursuit of the Boers was attempted they got clean away.

Colonel White's column, with the other half of No. 1 Company, had also marched from Thabanchu on hearing of the attack on Ladybrand, but when they arrived at Brakfontein information was received that the Boers had retired. The column was composed of 350 Imperial Yeomanry, the same number of infantry, and 2 guns. Colonel White at once sent the Imperial Yeomanry on to try and intercept the retreat. A detachment was ordered to proceed to Leeuw River Mills, and Sergeant Clarke, with 7 men of the 1st Company, proceeded to the village. This party was fired on from a house as it rode up, and lost two men, Private Garrett, who was shot through the neck, and killed, and Private Cory, shot throug the lung, who died the same afternoon. Sir Thomas Fowler, who was in command, galloped up with the supports at the noise of the firing, and the Boers, 14 in number, made off with the loss of 5 killed and 2 taken prisoners; so the two yeoman did not died unavenged. General Rundle meanwhile had moved to Bethlehem, the 3rd and 4th Companies being

with him; and General Campbell, with the 16th Brigade, 1900
was sent to Fouriesburg, while the 17th Brigade was ordered also up to Bethlehem from Vrede, Senekal being evacuated. Owing to the disturbed state of the country it was thought advisable to clear out the stores accumulated at Ficksburg. Colonel Golightly and No. 2 Company assisted at this duty, and the stores, together with a large amount of gold deposited at the Banks in the town, were removed across the border into Basutoland. After this the Wilts Company rejoined the 16th Brigade at Spitzkop, on September 9.

On September 5 the Thabanchu detachment rejoined the other half of the 1st Company at Ladybrand, and the whole marched, first to Leeuw River Mills, and thence to Thabanchu, arriving there on the 9th.

At Thabanchu the Company was served out with fresh horses, and on the 11th marched with Colonel White's column to Zand River and thence to Dornberg, this forming part of a movement designed to capture De Wet, but that wily general contrived to get away before the converging columns were in touch with each other.

No. 1 Company was then sent back to Zand River and thence to Winburg, where it arrived on September 24. The orders given to the Company originally were that it was to join the 8th Division at Senekal, but as troops were urgently needed to guard the railway it was retained in garrison at Winburg.

There for six months the 1st Company led a somewhat uneventful life, though there was plenty of work for it in the way of escorts for convoys, patrols, and expeditions to collect supplies.

On March 30 No. 1 was ordered to proceed by train to 1901
Harrismith to rejoin the Regimental Headquarters. The journey took seven days, as the train could only travel by

1901 day; and, indeed, the train was held up one day as it was by the line being blown up in front of it.

The 1st Company arrived at Harrismith on April 5, and rejoined the remainder of the regiment, and on the 12th was sent to Bloomfield Bridge, as a guard to the bridge. There it remained until orders were received to send the original Imperial Yeomanry home. The few that were left in the company, 48, left Harrismith on May 28, for Cape Town, where they embarked on the Roslyn Castle for England, and arrived at Southhampton on July 8.

1900 No. 2 Company had left Ficksburg at the end of August, and on September 3rd joined the 8th Division at Bethlehem, being attached to General Campbell's, the 16th, Brigade.

The Division was occupied in clearing the country between Bethlehem and Harrismith for the next ten days. On the 12th, Campbell's Brigade marched through Fourriesburg to Trommel, Macdonald being at Winburg and Bruce-Hamilton at Leeuw River Mills. On this day the Boers showed in force at Brandfort, whereupon, in pursuance of orders from General Kelly-Kenny at Bloemfontein General Macdonald crossed the Vet River, and in conjunction with General Campbell, attacked the enemy on the 13th at Tafel Kop. After some firing the enemy made off, dropping 31 wagons and 270 oxen; but only 7 prisoners were taken. There were no British casualties, though the Boers brought three guns into action.

On the 18th, General Rundle had another skirmish at Bronkhurstfontein near Bethlehem, taking one gun and 30 wagons. After which the Boers broke up into small parties and scattered among the hills, whereupon General Campbell returned to Bethlehem with No. 2 Company.

De Wet was now again at large in the Orange River

Colony, and Lord Roberts formed a fresh combination to 1900 deal with him.

The Colonial Division and De Lisle's Brigade were ordered to Rhenoster River, and four Infantry Brigades were detailed to support them and to converge on Lindley, namely those of Macdonald, Bruce-Hamilton, Boyes, and Campbell, which last was then at Reitz with, the 16th Brigade. The several Brigades marched accordingly, but the Boer Commandoes had contrived to slip through the cordon before the columns were in touch with each other, as usual.

The column was continuously sniped during the march, but beyond digging up a gun that was concealed at a farm, effected nothing, and on the 23rd General Campbell again returned to Bethlehem.

On the following day the column went out again.

On the 3rd October the enemy was encountered at Tafel Kop. A skirmish ensued in which No. 2 was engaged, but the company suffered no casualties, and on the 5th it returned to Vrede, where it remained in garrison till the 11th.

On the 7th October the 3rd and 4th Companies, with a few men of No. 2 Company, were sent to Standerton by rail to draw supplies. They returned to Vrede on the 11th, and had hardly got there when they were attacked by a party of the enemy just outside the town, whom they beat off, losing a sergeant killed and one private wounded.

On the 11th No. 2 again went on the trek with General Rundle, who marched to Reitz and thence to Bethlehem. On the 26th General Rundle marched out for Harrismith. A short distance out the enemy were discovered holding a strong position across the road. The I.Y. and two Companies of the Grenadier Guards were sent forward to turn the right flank of the position, while

1900 the rest of the Grenadiers made a frontal attack, whereupon the enemy broke and fled. The British loss in this action was 3 killed and 17 wounded, Private Carabine, of the 2nd Company, being among the latter.

On the 30th October the whole column again entered Harrismith, the 2nd Company having been sent to garrison Vrede. But these repeated and wearisome expeditions had little or no effect in pacifying the country, which, outside the garrisoned towns, was completely in the hands of the Boer Commandoes, and the British Generals were quite unable to deal with these for want of sufficient mounted men. Bloemfontein itself was practically besieged, while repeated attacks continued to be made on isolated posts throughout the Colony.

Thus, on the 15th October, Bulfontein was attacked, on the 18th Phillopolis, on the 19th Fauresmith, and on the 25th Jacobsdaal. The attacks on the first three places, which were garrisoned chiefly by the Yeomanry, were beaten off with considerable loss to the enemy, but Jacobsdaal, which was held by a detachment of Cape Town Highlanders, was taken by a night surprise, and though the place was re-occupied by supports from Orange River the next morning, and the few surviving men of the garrison who still obstinately held out in some houses rescued, the unfortunate Highlanders lost 26 men out of a total of 45. Harrismith and Vrede too, notwithstanding the presence of the 8th Division, were closely surrounded, and it was unsafe to venture beyond the lines of the picquets, and on the 23rd October No. 2 Company was engaged in a skirmish at Vrede in which Lieutenant Cavendish Browne and Private Martin were killed.

On the 15th November No. 2 marched to Harrismith,
1901 where it remained in garrison until the 27th January 1901, on which date it was detailed, with a detachment of

Grenadiers, as a guard over the Bloomfield railway-bridge, 1901
under the command of Captain Speke.

The company remained at the bridge for the next six weeks, when it was ordered back to Harrismith, being then commanded by Lieutenant Hugh Speke, Captain Speke having been sent into hospital suffering from enteric fever.

On the 6th April Lieutenant Thornton returned from sick furlough and took over command of the company, which was now mainly composed of the second contingent of Imperial Yeomanry, very few of the original men being left.

A general "Boer drive" was now organized in the north of the Orange River Colony, in which upwards of 10,000 men were engaged, and General Rundle was ordered to co-operate with this force by a series of operations in the south-east. Large as the British force seemed on paper, it was nevertheless quite insufficient to effectually cover the extent of country embraced in the operations, this comprising over 10,000 square miles. Beyond the capture of a quantity of cattle and wagons it accomplished but little, as the Boer Commandoes easily evaded the British columns.

General Rundle himself, with General Campbell's Brigade and the 2nd, 3rd and 4th Companies of the 1st I.Y., now under command of Colonel Keir, R.H.A., left Harrismith on the 19th April, Vrede being evacuated. The Division first marched to Bethlehem, harassed throughout by the enemy, who hung persistently to the flanks and rear. On the 23rd No. 2 fought a stiffly-contested rear-guard action at Tiger's Kloof, accounting for 24 of the enemy, and losing two killed and nine wounded.

On the 29th General Rundle entered the Brandwater Basin by way of Retiefs Nek, and on the 2nd May the

1901 Division occupied Fourriesburg. Here the Division split up into small columns, which scoured the surrounding country, clearing out the farms, burning mills, and collecting sheep and cattle.

At the end of May, in pursuance of the orders for the recall of the men of the original Imperial Yeomanry, the three Companies of the 1st Regiment I.Y. were sent back to Harrismith, where they arrived on the 10th June, and on the 12th the few remaining men left in the 2nd Company entrained for Cape Town. They were delayed for six days at De Aar, and on the 27th they embarked on board the ss. Manchester Merchant and sailed for England.

The transport arrived at Southampton on the 19th July, one man, Private Rugg, having died four days out of the port of enteric fever.

CHAPTER XXVI.

The 63rd Company.

The 63rd Company arrived at Pretoria on the 15th 1900 August, and was at once posted to the Brigade under Colonel Hickman, which formed part of General Paget's command. During the following week the Company was employed in patrol duties on the western side of Pretoria. Lord Roberts now decided to send a strong force to clear the line of railway running north from Pretoria to Pietersburg, and on the 22nd the 63rd left by train for Waterval, where it joined General Baden-Powell. Generals Paget and Baden-Powell marched from Waterval along the line of railway, while on the left of the advance General Ian Hamilton operated from the Crocodile River. Lord Roberts himself intended to resume the offensive in the Eastern Transvaal, and designed this movement along the railway in order to divert the enemy's attention from that part of the country.

The line of march was through the so-called "Bushveldt", a species of jungle which afforded excellent cover to the Boers. There was continuous sniping by small parties that hung persistently to the flanks of the column, and several patrols lost their way in the thick bush and were cut off and taken by the enemy.

On the 24th the rear-guard of the retreating Boer commando, under Grobler, was overtaken at Hamman's Kraal. This was at once attacked, and some sharp fighting took place, the Rhodesian Horse, which was charged by a number of mounted Boers, losing Colonel Spreckley and four men killed, and eight wounded in a hand-to-hand combat.

1900 The next day the railway-crossing over the Pienaar River was reached, but the enemy had previously blown up the bridge. Thence the column moved to Warmbads, and drove out the Boers, who were in considerable force, capturing 25 men and liberating 100 British prisoners. Nylstrow was then occupied, where a large quantity of stores were captured, after which the enemy broke up into small parties and scattered in the Bush.

On the 28th the 63rd returned to Warmbads, to which General Hamilton now moved, being followed by Generals Paget and Clements; but Lord Roberts needing troops for his intended advance along the Delagoa Bay railway, he recalled Hamilton to Pretoria, sent Clements to Krugersdorp, and left General Baden-Powell to continue the operations, the 63rd being left to garrison Warmbads.

Here the 63rd was practically besieged until General Plumer came in on the 5th September, and on the following day the Company retired with him to Pienaar River and thence to Waterval.

The 63rd took part in several small expeditions for the purpose of clearing the enemy out of the Bush-Veldt, which were not attended by any great success though there was a good deal of desultory fighting, until the 14th October when it returned to Pretoria.

There the Company was again employed in similar duties in the neighbourhood of the town. On the 25th the proclamation announcing the annexation of the Transvaal was read by the Governor in the great square in the presence of the whole garrison, including the 63rd, and the Royal Standard hoisted to a salute of 21 guns, after which the troops marched past and saluted the flag.

On the 4th November the 63rd returned to Waterval, where it rested until December 19th, when the Company was sent out to Hebron and Bethanie to round up some

wandering parties of Boers, returning on Christmas Day 1900
with 30 prisoners. On the 29th the Company again left
to take part in a movement against Delarey, and after an
extended march round the Magaliesburg returned to
Pretoria on January 17th. 1901

A combined movement was now ordered against Louis Botha, who was giving much trouble in the Eastern Transvaal. The 63rd was attached to the Brigade under Colonel Jefferies in General Plumer's column, and sent by train to Balmoral. But these operations were scarcely commenced when the urgent necessity of stopping De Wet, then in the Orange River Colony, from invading Cape Colony, necessitated their temporary suspension. General Plumer's force was ordered to entrain at Balmoral, and was brought to Naauwport, on the borders of Cape Colony, having traversed the whole of the Orange River Colony on its way, and on February 11th the Brigade reached Coleberg. By this time De Wet had escaped from Generals Knox and Bruce-Hamilton, who had attempted to intercept him before he could cross the Orange River, and this extended and circuitous movement of the troops by rail was intended to place a strong force still further south and again to bar his way.

On the 8th February De Wet was reported to be at Philippolis. While in this neighbourhood he had collected a large number of horses and a quantity of supplies from the Fouriesburg district, which was now entirely in the hands of the Boers. His force amounted to 3,000 men with seven guns. He expected to be joined by several commandoes, now at large in the north of Cape Colony, as soon as he had crossed the Orange River to the number of at least 2,000 more men, and with this considerable strength he hoped to accomplish the invasion of Cape Colony and cut the British line of communications.

1901 There were already several marauding commandoes under Kritziger, Lotter, Malan, and others at large in the Colony, which were receiving every possible assistance and encouragement from the rebellious Dutch population of the Cape, and there was no doubt that if these desultory operations could be conducted by a general of De Wet's capacity at the head of a compact force of 5,000 seasoned men the situation would be extremely serious. All other operations therefore were suspended so that a vigorous effort might be made to frustrate De Wet's intentions. For this purpose some 20,000 men were rapidly moved to the Orange River frontiers. General Lyttleton, who had charge of the operations, had his head-quarters at De Aar. General Bruce-Hamilton was moved by train from Bloemfontein to Bethulie on the Orange River, Crabbe and Henniker were at De Aar, General Knox threatened Philippolis, south of De Aar Bethune's Cavalry Brigade was at Richmond Road, Haig's column at Frazerburg Road, and further south was General Paget at Victoria West; while to the west De Lisle occupied Carnarvon, and another British force Prieska.

On the morning of the 10th February De Wet crossed the Orange River at Zand Drift, and moved south to Hamelfontein, about ten miles north of Colesburg, where the next day he was promptly attacked by General Plumer's advance guard, with which was the 63rd Company.

De Wet now turned off to the north-west, hotly pursued by Plumer, who, on the 14th, engaged his rear-guard at Wolvekuil, or Wolvehoek (the name is variously given). The weather had now become extremely bad. Deluges of rain fell without intermission, rapidly converting the veldt into a vast quagmire, and rendering the movements of both the British and the Boers difficult. Both sides, however, pressed on to the utmost of their ability, De Wet

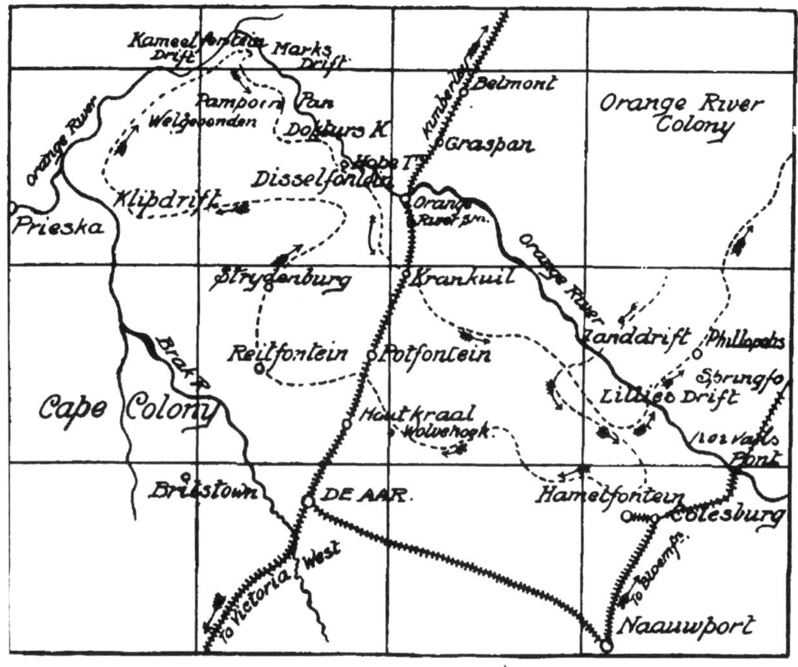

Map to illustrate the De Wet Hunt in Cape Colony, February, 1901.
De Wet's march is indicated by the dotted lines.

This Map is divided into 40-mile squares.

trying to escape from the grasp of his pertinacious adversary, and Plumer hanging on the retreating foe with bull-dog obstinacy, notwithstanding his great inferiority of strength. 1901

In the afternoon of the 14th, Plumer at last sighted the whole Boer force scarcely four miles away, and now laagered up. Preparations were made for an immediate attack and a decisive action appeared inevitable, when one of the tremendous hail-storms, for which South Africa is noted, preceded, as usual, by a strong wind and thick clouds of dust, came down with terrific violence. The attack was, perforce, suspended until the storm had somewhat abated, but when the weather cleared, which was not until it was getting dusk, De Wet had disappeared with his army. It was impossible for the weary troops to pursue him further, though some pursuit was indeed attempted. It was growing dark, the ground, saturated by the storm, was well-nigh impassable, and the column, perforce, bivouacked in the wet and cold for the night.

At day-break on the 15th the chase was renewed. De Wet and his men had got by this time a good lead, and had crossed the railway a few miles below Potfontein, still heading west. The Boer transport, however, could not be dragged through the heavy rain-soaked veldt, and in the course of the day 40 wagons, with a large quantity of ammunition, a Maxim gun, and 30 prisoners were taken. This day Bruce-Hamilton contrived with some difficulty to cross the swollen Orange River at Zand Drift and moved on De Aar, while Henniker's column marched from Philipstown on Houtkraal. De Wet was now reported to be at Rietfontein with his main body. Here, after a short rest, his force divided up into several parts, making towards Strydenburg.

On the 17th Plumer, who had left his transport to

1901 follow him as best it could, again overtook De Wet's rear-guard early in the morning of the 17th. Jefferies and the mounted men at once attacked the enemy, surprising them at breakfast, and drove them off in utter rout, pursuing them until the complete failure of all supplies and the exhaustion of the horses compelled a halt.

Plumer had now completely lost the trail, as nothing could be seen of the enemy. De Wet had, in fact, been headed off from his march west-ward, and having abruptly turned north was now making for Hope Town, where he expected to be rejoined by the other commandoes, and to obtain a supply of provisions and horses. The 63rd and 100 Australians were sent forward, under Colonel Vials, to try and pick up the scent, and on the 22nd had the good fortune to locate the enemy at Kameel's Drift, on the Orange River, where De Wet had laagered for the night.

De Wet had, it appeared, attempted to re-cross the river near Hope Town, but though a few of his men succeeded in swimming across, some were swept away by the swollen torrent and drowned. He therefore abandoned the attempt; and turning due west made for Prieska, hoping to cross the Brak River at Klip Drift. The Brak also was in full flood when he reached the Drift, and finding that several of the British columns were in the neighbourhood, he hurriedly turned north again and made two desperate but unsuccessful efforts to cross into the Orange River Colony, first at Kameel's Drift and then at Mark's Drift.

Plumer had halted for the night at Welgevonden, some 22 miles south of the Boer position, where he had been joined by Henniker's column. Here, Colonel Viall's message found him, and at dawn he started at once with the combined columns, Colonel Vialls in the mean time trying to hold the enemy with his small force.

De Wet now made off up the river towards Hope Town, 1901
but Plumer's advance guard came up with him at Pampoens Pan, 15 miles from Kameel's Drift. The enemy, who held a strong position on a long ridge, running east and west, brought a pompom into action, and looked like making a stand, but being at once vigorously attacked by Crabbe and Henniker, who led the advance, broke and fled in every direction, casting away their arms, ammunition, and equipment, and losing forty men prisoners.

The pursuit was kept up with great vigour. Towards evening the Boer camp was sighted at Disselfontein, and two guns could be seen near it. Without any hesitation Colonel Marker, of the Coldstreams, led the Victorian Horse straight for the guns, followed at headlong speed by the 63rd and the Imperial Light Horse. The Boers fled in confusion, and the guns, a 15-pounder and a pompom, were taken. Colonel Owen, with a squadron of the 1st Dragoon Guards, continued the pursuit until nightfall, capturing the Boer camp, with its kettles and equipment. De Wet, who now had with him about 1,200 men, and was still accompanied by his inseparable companion, ex-President Steyn, continued his flight during the night, working round to the south of Hope Town.

Early in the morning of the 24th the fugitives crossed the railway at Kraankuil, and this being reported to General Lyttleton, all the columns were directed to converge upon Zand Drift, where De Wet was expected to try to re-cross the river.

De Wet kept his course along the river, which was now slowly falling, seeking a practicable crossing, and on the 27th his capture by the numerous converging columns seemed inevitable. But by some mistake Colonel Byng, who was to have closed and completed the circle from

1901 Colesberg, was ordered to retire instead of advancing, just at the critical moment. The wary and watchful Boer General at once grasped the opportunity. He slipped through the gap thus created without the loss of a moment, and finding the ford at Lilliefontein passable, crossed early on the 28th, and effected his escape into the Orange River Colony with 1,500 men, losing a few men on the passage from the fire of a patrol of Nesbit's Horse who witnessed the crossing, but whom the Boers did not stop to fight, and leaving behind them five carts and a number of horses. Thus ended the great De Wet hunt from which so much had been expected.

Though the British force failed to capture him, De Wet's expedition had been anything but a success. His projected invasion had been summarily stopped; he had lost 250 men, all his carts and wagons, and two of his guns; while his men, who had been hunted continuously for three weeks, were in the last stages of distress and exhaustion. That he could have been, and ought to have been, taken is certain, but the fault certainly did not lie with the active and energetic Plumer and his indefatigable horsemen, who had hung like wild cats on to the enemy from start to finish, though barely a third of his numbers.

Meanwhile, General Plumer's worn-out column[1] had stopped at Hope Town to refit, and as soon as this was completed the troops were entrained and moved to Springfontein, between Bloemfontein and Norval's Pont. Here they detrained and marched to Philippolis, again on the track of their old enemy De Wet.

The column reached Philippolis on the 3rd March, and the next day engaged De Wet's rear-guard at Zuurfontein without any decisive results. The pursuit was continued

[1] The troops had marched 350 miles in 13 days in the most dreadful weather.

as far as Brandfort, where the column arrived on 1901
March 11th. De Wet's force had now broken up into small parties, and further pursuit being regarded as hopeless, the 63rd was sent back to Bloemfontein, where it rested from the 16th to the 24th March.

On the 25th March the 63rd joined Colonel Byng's column, which formed part of the force under General Bruce-Hamilton, who was ordered to commence a series of operations in the south-east of the Orange River Colony intended to settle this district, which had been for some time entirely in the hands of the Boers under Fourie, who had refused to follow De Wet across the Orange River. The column traversed the district for three weeks, taking prisoners and collecting cattle and horses. There was little fighting of consequence, though the columns were continuously sniped, the principal achievement being the combat at Rietspruit Farm, on the 11th April, which place Bethune's Horse stormed and captured, taking Commandant Bresler and 83 men.

On the 15th May orders were received that the men of the original Imperial Yeomanry were to go home at once. On the 16th the 63rd was entrained at Prior's Siding for Worcester, and thence the Company was sent to Cape Town, where, on the 25th, it embarked on the *Tintagel Castle* and sailed for home, landing at Southampton on the 11th June.

The 63rd was singularly fortunate throughout the campaign, in that, though continuously in the field for over a year, with the exception of the short time spent in garrison at Waterval, and under fire almost daily, it did not lose an officer or man killed in action, though several men were wounded. The losses by disease also were remarkably few, amounting during the year to one sergeant-major (Holliday) and two privates (J. Young and W. J. Blandford).

APPENDIX TO CHAPTER XXVI.

A ROLL of the OFFICERS, N. C. O.'s, and MEN of the 1st, 2nd, and 63rd Companies, Staff and Gun Section of the First Battalion Imperial Yeomanry who died or were killed in action in South Africa.

NO. 1 COMPANY:—

Captain Sir Thomas Fowler, killed 20th April 1902.
Sergeant F. W. Butler, died 8th July 1900.
Shoeing-smith A. Urch, died 25th November 1900.
Private Briggs, T. G., died 27th January 1901.
„ Butler, W., died 23rd February 1901.
„ Cory, R. V., killed 4th September 1900.
„ Dobbie, W. H., killed 31st October 1901.
„ Davies, G., killed 20th April 1902.
„ Davies, J., died 16th July 1901.
„ Garrett, W. E., killed 6th December 1900.
„ Goodman, C. H., killed 11th November 1900.
„ Hill, E. J., died 25th December 1900.
„ Iles, R. W., died 20th June 1900.
„ Jones, J , died 11th March 1902.
„ Lloyd, A. P., died 3rd July 1900.
„ McCarthy, D., killed 20th April 1902.
„ Nicholson, T. B , died 27th July 1900.
„ Prophit, W. C., died 31st March 1901.
„ Smelt, A. H., died 19th December 1901.
„ Thomas, C. O , killed 27th April 1902.
Lance-Corporal Wood, L. C., died 21st March 1901.

NO. 2 COMPANY:—

Captain W. W S. Clarke, killed 26th August 1900.
Lieutenant J. C. Browne, killed 23rd October 1900.
Q -M.-Sergeant Temperton, J. H., died 8th March 1902.
Sergeant Butcher, G. J., died 6th February 1901.
Corporal Carey, H., died 9th December 1900.
Private Brown, J. A., killed 20th August 1900.

Private Bushell, G. E. H., died 26th August 1900.
„ Daniells, C. W., died 9th January 1901.
„ Dent, W., died 6th December 1900.
„ Featherstone, C. J., died 24th March 1901.
„ Jefferys, J. W., died 13th February 1901.
„ King, F. C., died 9th June 1900.
„ Lynn, A., killed 2nd February 1901.
„ Lewis, F., died 21st January 1901.
„ Marden, B. J., killed 25th October 1900.
„ Rugg, J., died 4th March 1901.
„ Wheeler, H. C., died 21st May 1900.
„ Young, F. W., killed 20th August 1900.

NO. 63 COMPANY

Lieutenant M. Hastings, killed 10th November 1901.
Serg.-Major Holliday, E. J., died 19th January 1901.
Sergeant Smith, F., died 18th November 1901.
Bugler Keeling, E. E., died 21st February 1902.
Private Blandford, W. J., died 22nd August 1900.
„ Harvey, E. R., died 5th March 1902.
„ O'Hare, W. J., died 11th April 1902.
„ Perry, W., died 2nd December 1901
„ Young, J., died 16th January 1901.

LIST OF WOUNDED:—

Private F. Dean, Gun Section, 28th July 1900.
Sergeant R Harrington, Gun Section, 28th July 1900.
Sergeant-Major Lyford, No. 1, 3rd September 1900.
Lance-Corpl. H. B. Burnaby, No. 1, 7th November 1900.
Private J. A. Norris, No. 1, 8th October 1900.
Private Simkins, No. 1, 4th September 1900.
Sergeant G. Butcher, No. 1, 2nd October 1900.
Private J. Coombs, No. 1, 2nd October 1900.
Corporal W. Dean, No. 1, 20th August 1900.
Private G. Sparrow, No. 1, 20th August 1900
„ J. Hill, No. 1, 24th August 1900.
„ G. Howe, No. 1, 21st November 1900.
„ F. Carabine, No. 1, 26th October 1900.
„ W. L. D. Strother, No. 63, 24th August 1900.

CHAPTER XXVII.

1900 The war in Africa gave the usual stimulus to recruiting, and in 1900 no less than 183 new recruits were added to the Regimental Muster Roll. Throughout the history of the regiment a war always brought a large increase in the strength. Even the Crimean War, little as it possibly could affect the Home Forces, was no exception, and now that the great value of the Yeomanry was fully recognised a very much greater interest in the force was the natural consequence, combined with a desire to make the training a much more business-like proceeding than in former years. After the excitement of the Trowbridge training and the temporary loss of the services of those Yeomen who had joined the Service Squadrons, it was thought advisable to hold the Permanent Duty in the autumn instead of the spring, and to hold it under canvass. The regiment accordingly assembled for the training on the 3rd of September, at West Down, Colonel W. H. Long being in command. The places of the absent officers had previously been filled up, and a Regimental Quartermaster, Lieutenant Hooper Deacon, appointed, making a total of 31 officers. Under the new Regulations the old eight days' training was this year for the first time extended to three weeks, and this, combined with the invaluable experience gained by a camp life, effected a very marked improvement in the efficiency of the regiment. Musketry practice was carried out during the training at the Shrewton ranges, and the challenge cup competed for, this being won by Trooper Harding, of the Malmesbury Troop.

The regiment took part in a field day with the other troops in camp on Salisbury Plain on the 14th, being told off to hold the line of the Avon from Netheravon to Durrington against an attacking force, which duty was very ably performed. 1900

The Inspection by General Clarke was held on the 18th. The regiment showed a total strength of 349 officers and men, being 25 over the establishment, there being 11 officers and 54 rank and file absent in South Africa.

On the 3rd of September the following Order was published with reference to the deaths of two officers, Sir Henry Bruce Meux, and Sir Algernon Neeld, who had died since the training of 1899 :—

"The O.C. deeply regrets that since last Permanent Duty the Regiment has been deprived by death of the services of two of its officers.

"Major and Hon. Lieutenant-Colonel Sir H. B. Meux commanded the Malmesbury Troop for many years, and always did his best to make it efficient and up to strength, and his death is a subject of deep regret.

"Major and Lieutenant-Colonel Sir Algernon Neeld was Second in Command of the Regiment, after having commanded the Chippenham Troop. As an officer and friend he earned for himself the respect and affection of all who knew him, and his loss must be deeply felt by all ranks. He never failed to do his duty with all his might, and has left an example which all will do well to follow."

Kharki helmets were served out for the first time this year, and the regiment, also for the first time, was exercised in "Field Firing" during the training.

During this year the negotiations that resulted in the union of all the Australian Colonies into one Government, to be styled the Commonwealth of Australia, were brought to a successful conclusion. The proclamation of the union was fixed for the 1st January 1901, the commencement of the new century offering a fitting date for the inauguration of so auspicious an event.

Her Majesty the Queen was pleased to direct that a

1900 representative contingent drawn from each of the various branches of the Service should attend the ceremony, and the R. Wiltshire, as the Premier Regiment of Yeomanry Cavalry in Great Britain, had the honour to be called on to provide the Yeomanry Detachment, consisting of 2 officers, 2 sergeants, and 27 rank and file. When this was notified in Orders 70 applications were sent in. These, however, were eventually reduced to 41, and the candidates were ordered to parade for inspection at Trowbridge.

A committee of officers under the presidency of Colonel W. H. Long was appointed to perform the very difficult and somewhat invidious task of selecting the required number out of these, which was done after a very lengthy and tedious inspection.

Major Goddard was appointed to command, with 2nd Lieutenant W. F. Fuller as subaltern officer. The men selected were afterwards inspected by General Sir Baker Russell, G. O. C. Southern District, and sworn in as specially enlisted soldiers.

On the 12th November the various detachments, now forming the "Imperial Representative Corps," as it was styled officially, embarked on board the ss. Britannic at Southampton and sailed the same afternoon.

The Corps was under the command of Lieutenant-Colonel W. G. Crole-Wyndham, C.B., 21st Lancers, with Captain A. H. E. Wood, 2nd Scottish Rifles, as adjutant. It was composed of 25 N.C.O.'s and men each from the Household Brigade Cavalry, and 1st Dragoon Guards, 7th Hussars and 21st Lancers, 58 men R.H.A. V Battery, 57 R.F.A. 10th Battery, 46 R.G.A., 56 R.E., with 24 N.C.O.'s and men from each regiment of Foot Guards and 24 each from sixteen regiments of the Line. There were also detachments of the A.S.C., R.A.M.C., A.O.C., A.P.D., the 4th Norfolk Militia Regiment, the Vol. Batt. Devon

Regiment and 1st Middlesex Vol. Rifle Corps. The Cavalry 1900 took their saddlery with them, the gun detachment 2 guns and one wagon each, the R.E. a section of a pontoon train, telegraph section and balloon section, the Highland Light Infantry Regiment supplied the band, and the Royal and the Seaforth Highlanders a piper each. The men received pay and rations at Army rates. Arrangements were made in Australia to provide the necessary horses for the mounted sections.

The *Britannic* touched at Gibraltar on the 17th November, but did not remain long enough for anyone to land. On the 20th the ship arrived at Malta early in the morning and anchored in the Grand Harbour.

Soon afterwards the Governor, Sir Francis Grenfell, boarded the ship and was received with a Royal Salute. The corps then landed and marched to the Palace Square where it was inspected by Admiral Fisher, Commander-in-Chief of the Mediterranean Fleet. After viewing the Palace, the troops marched back by a circuitous route through the streets of Valetta, and having re-embarked, resumed their voyage in the afternoon.

The Governor and Commander-in-Chief issued an Order before the ship sailed expressing his satisfaction at having been able to receive the corps, congratulating the troops on their smartness, and wishing them a pleasant voyage. The ship coaled at Port Said, and again at Aden, and after an uneventful voyage on the 13th December anchored off Freemantle in West Australia, and the next day, the 14th, entered the harbour. It was not intended originally to disembark the troops here, and consequently there was some disappointment when they did land owing to Kharki being worn. This, however, was unavoidable, as the full dress kits were stowed away and could not be got at in time.

1900 The troops disembarked at mid-day, and were enthusiastically greeted by a large crowd. The Freemantle Artillery and Infantry, with their band, were drawn up to receive them, and, headed by the Mayor, the whole force marched through Freemantle to the Drill Hall, where the first of the many magnificent feeds provided by the hospitable Australians was partaken of. The Mayor made a short speech of welcome, and called for three cheers for the Queen, which was acknowledged by Colonel Crole-Wyndham in suitable terms. The corps then marched to the station, and at 2.30 p.m. took the train for Perth.

At Perth the troops were met at the station by the Premier, Sir J. Forrest, and after marching through the city were entertained at dinner in the Drill Hall, His Excellency, the Administrator, Sir A. Onslow, presiding. After the usual loyal speeches the troops again marched through the town to the station and returned to Freemantle where they embarked. The next day the ship sailed at 8.30 a.m. for Sydney, New South Wales.

On the morning of the 22nd the *Britannic* anchored in Sydney Harbour, and found the *Dalhousie*, with the Indian contingent, already there. This corps was 100 strong, made up of men selected from representative troops of the Indian Native Army.

The troops landed at 2.30 p.m., and were marched at once to the Victoria Barracks. On arrival there the men were formed up in the barrack square, where they were inspected by the Earl of Hopetown, the new Governor-General designate, who was attended by Major-General French the Commander-in-Chief, and several of the principal Ministers of State.

The men were then dismissed to their quarters, some to the Barracks and the rest to the Agricultural Grounds, where every preparation that could conduce to their comfort had been made. The day was very hot and damp, very trying to men fresh from a long voyage, and after the hard work of disembarking kits, etc., in the morning, all were very glad to retire to rest. 1900

The next day being Sunday, parade services were held in barracks. On Monday the horses were served out, and the afternoon was spent in endeavouring to impart the rudiments of military education to the new mounts, an operation attended by disastrous results to many of the riders. Christmas Day and Boxing Day were observed as holidays, and during the rest of the month the men were fully occupied in training the horses and accustoming them to what in riding school language is termed "sights and sounds", an operation which caused the greatest possible amusement to the crowds of spectators who anxiously watched the proceedings; and in attending the numerous dinners and entertainments provided by the hospitable citizens of Sydney.

At last the eventful day came that inaugurated the 1901
commencement of the new century and the birth of the Australian nation by the establishment of the Australian Commonwealth.

The troops, and the carriages that were to take part in the procession, were ordered to parade in the great park, known as the Domain, at 9.30 a.m. After an hour had been occupied in marshalling the component parts of the procession the bugles sounded the march, and the troops, headed by the Commander-in-Chief, moved off, exactly an hour elapsing before the last of the troops filed off through the gates opposite the Cathedral.

The procession was headed by 200 mounted police. After whom followed in order:—

1. The Trade Union Representatives and Friendly Societies.

1901 **2. The Fire Brigade with their engines.**

3. The Press.

4. The Italian Car.

5. The Canadian Car.

6. The Church, Mayors of Australian Cities, Premiers and Ministers of State of the several Colonies, Judges, and members of the Civil Service.

7. The Military Contingents in the following order:—

New South Wales Lancers.
Public School Cadets.
Troops returned from S. Africa.
Soudan Contingent.
Retired officers and men of H.M. Services.
Detachments of Infantry from each of the Australasian Colonies.
The Indian Contingent.
The Imperial Representative Corps.
Visiting Officers and Local Commandants.
Aides-de-Camp of G.O.C.
New South Wales Headquarter Staff.
Major-General French, G.O.C.
Admiral Pearson, Naval Commander-in-Chief and Staff.
Escort of Lancers.
Staff Officers of the Governor-General.
H.E. The Governor-General.
Escort of Lancers.

The procession proceeded through the City by way of Queen's Square, Macquarie Street, Bridge Street, Pitt Street, Park Street, Oxford Street, and Glenmore Road, to the Centennial Park, where the ceremony of swearing in the new Governor-General was to take place, passing successively under magnificent arches erected by the French, United States, and Germany, in honour of the occasion, The whole route was beautifully decorated, there being many other arches, of which those known as the Wool and the Wheat arches were the most remarkable, and was lined throughout by crowds of enthusiastic spectators. In the Centennial Park a white pavilion of classic design had been prepared, in which was placed the elaborate gilt table and inkstand which H.M. The Queen had used when giving her assent to the Act constituting the Commonwealth of Australia, and a fine block of Australian marble, destined to become the "Coronation Stone" of the Commonwealth, on which the Governor-General was to stand during the ceremony. 1901

The procession filed into the Park and the troops formed line opposite the Pavilion, where Lord Hopetown was received by the Premier of New South Wales, Sir Wm. Lyne, and the Lieut.-Governor, Sir F. Darley. On the arrival of Lord Hopetown the R. Australian Artillery fired a salute of 19 guns and the National Anthem was played by the massed bands. As the one o'clock gun fired, His Excellency stepped into the pavilion and took his place on the Commonweath Stone.

The Ceremony then commenced with a hymn, sung by the choir of St. Andrews, and after a special prayer had been said by the Archbishop, the Queen's Proclamation and the Letters Patent establishing the Commonwealth were read by Mr. Blackmore.

His Excellency then took the Oath of Allegiance and the Oaths of Office, and by these acts consummated the Union of Australia.

A salute of 21 guns, followed by a tremendous outburst of cheering signalized the completion of this momentous event. His Excellency's Proclamation notifying his assumption of the office of Governor-General was read as soon as the cheering had subsided. The Federal ministers were then sworn in, and the singing of the Te Deum by

1901 the choir of 400 voices brought a most impressive ceremony to a fitting close.

His Excellency then read messages of congratulation from H.M. the Queen and the Imperial Government, and after bowing to the people from each side of the pavilion, re-entered his carriage amidst the roar of another salute from the artillery, and drove away with his escort. The massed choirs of the Public Schools to the number of 10,000 children then sung the "Federated Australia" chorus with great effect. This was followed by the "Hallelujah Chorus" by 1,000 adult voices, and after "God save the Queen" had been sung by the whole assembly the proceedings came to a close, the crowds of spectators dispersed, and the troops returned to quarters.

A State Banquet was given in the Town Hall in the evening, which was attended by the officers of the Imperial Representative Corps, and upwards of 1,000 guests. The Governor-General was unable to preside from fatigue, so the chair was taken by the Lieut.-Governor of New South Wales. The usual loyal toasts were proposed, and Colonel Crole-Wyndham, in returning thanks on behalf of the Army and Volunteers, made a remarkably fine speech. The town was illuminated in a very beautiful and impressive manner on this and the following seven nights.

On the 2nd the Highland Society held its Annual Gathering, and entertained the officers to lunch in the interval between the sports, at which the members of the I.R.C., who competed, were singularly successful, winning seven events, including the gold medal for the piping competition. In the evening a Naval and Military Tattoo was given in the Agricultural Grounds by the bands of all the various corps quartered in the city, 20 in number.

On the 3rd H.E. The Governor-General reviewed the whole of the troops in the Centennial Park. There

were present on parade 555 officers, 181 warrant officers 1901
and sergeants, 8,873 rank and file, 34 guns and 1,819 horses. The march past was led by the R.H.A., followed by the cavalry of the I.R. Corps. After the march past the Cavalry Brigade formed line and advancing in review order, under command of Colonel Crole-Wyndham, gave the Royal Salute.

The Governor-General afterwards issued a very complimentary order to the troops as also did General French, who specially thanked Colonel Crole-Wyndham for his efficient handling of the Cavalry Brigade.

On the 4th there was a display of fireworks by the fleet and shipping in the harbour, and on the 5th a great Naval and Military Banquet was given in the Town Hall by the New South Wales Government. Here Colonel Crole-Wyndham gave another excellent speech, which was greatly applauded.

On the 7th and 8th an Assault-at-Arms and Naval and Military Sports were held in the Agricultural Grounds, in which the I.R.C. and the Indian contingent took part.

The proceedings closed with a most interesting and realistic representation of the assault and capture of an Indian hill fort.

On the 12th the Citizen's Committee entertained the Imperial troops and the Naval Squadron at a Smoking Concert, which was closed by a vote of thanks to the Mayor and citizens by Colonel Crole-Wyndham, and the Sydney festivites came to an end.

On the 14th the troops paraded at 11.30 a.m. and marched to the harbour for embarkation, Lord Hopetown, attended by the Federal Premier, the Premier of New South Wales, the Colonial Secretary, the Mayor of Sydney, and other leading personages went down to the *Britannic* to bid farewell to Colonel Crole-Wyndham and the I.R.C.

1901 Colonel McKenzie, A.A.G., read out on parade a special general order in which the Governor-General expressed his pleasure and satisfaction at having been present at the review on the 7th. The troops who had been paraded on the wharf to receive the Governor-General, who made a short farewell speech to them, then embarked, and at 4 p.m. the *Britannic* left the quay and sailed for Brisbane, in Queensland.

Early in the morning of the 16th, the *Britannic* anchored in Moreton Bay, about 20 miles below the city of Brisbane, and in the afternoon the Cavalry and Artillery sent up parties to take over horses and fit saddlery.

The *Dalhousie* had already arrived with the Indian contingent, having left Sydney some hours before the *Britannic*, and being able to cross the bar owing to her lighter draught, had proceeded direct up the river to Brisbane.

The officers, who were quartered in the Parliament House and the Queensland Club, were entertained at dinner by the Governor, Lord Lamington, in the evening.

On the following day the troops went up to Brisbane and paraded in the Domain Park at 10.30 a.m., where they received an address of welcome from the Premier, Mr. Philp, a copy of which, handsomely bound, was handed to Colonel Crole-Wyndham.

After suitable acknowledgements, the I.R.C. and the Indian contingent moved off in column of route, passing through the Government House grounds where H.E. The Governor received the salute. They were followed by the Queensland contingent, which had returned the day before from South Africa, and the local troops.

After marching through the city, which was gaily decorated in their honour, the I.R.C. filed on to the race course, where dinner was provided for the men and lunch for the officers. In the afternoon military sports and jumping competitions were held, after which the troops returned to the jetty and were sent back in two tenders to the *Britannic*. In the evening the officers were entertained at dinner by the Queensland Club. 1901

The following day was spent pleasantly in sight-seeing and amusements of various descriptions, the troops embarking late at night. Early on the morning of the 19th the *Britannic* sailed for Tasmania, leaving 14 men behind, who missed the tenders owing to some mistake about the time. These were sent on to Melbourne by train to rejoin the corps there. The voyage lasted four days, and late in the evening of the 22nd the ship anchored at Hobart.

Here the corps received the melancholy intelligence of the fatal illness of H.M. the Queen. The news came as a great shock to all, as it was totally unexpected. Late at night a second message was delivered to the effect that Her Majesty was actually dying, and when the troops disembarked the next morning they were met by the news that our beloved Queen was dead.

All festivities were of course at once abandoned. The remainder of the day was spent quietly on shore by those who had friends in the town, but most of the men had no heart for any amusement and returned to the ship.

The following day at 10 a.m. the troops paraded for Divine Service and marched through Hobart to the Domain, where they found the local forces already assembled, together with a great number of the citizens, who stood in crowds on the slopes of the surrounding hills.

All the military chaplains, irrespective of creed, took part in a most impressive service. The Tasmanian chaplain commenced by reading the opening sentences of

1901 the Burial Service. The Presbyterian chaplain to the I.R.C., the Rev. T. H. Chapman, then followed with the 90th Psalm, and the Wesleyan chaplain to the corps, the Rev. R. W. Allen, read the lesson. After a hymn had been sung, the senior chaplain to the Tasmanian forces read the closing collects of the burial service, and the R.C. chaplain to the I.R.C. offered up a prayer.

After an address by the Rev. A. E. Townend, senior chaplain to the I.R.C., a hymn was sung, followed by the "Dead March" played by the massed bands. The troops then marched back to the ship. In the afternoon the Mayors of Launceston and Hobart, and the Premier of Tasmania, Mr. Elliot Lewis, came on board, and expressed the great regret and disappointment they felt at the curtailment of the welcome prepared for the I.R.C., necessitated by the sad loss the empire had sustained. The ship sailed shortly afterwards for Melbourne. On Saturday morning, the 26th, in dull, rainy weather, the *Britannic* entered Port Melbourne and was berthed alongside of the railway pier.

Like Hobart, Melbourne was in deep mourning, the flags half-mast, and the public buildings draped in black. The next morning, Sunday, the troops paraded for Divine Service, and taking the train to Spencer Street, marched from the station by way of Collins Street to the Exhibition Buildings, a distance of two miles. The interior of the building was hung with black muslin relieved by knots of Imperial purple. The nave and transepts were filled with troops, and the gallery with civilians in deep mourning. On a central platform, draped with black and purple, were the officiating Clergy and Officers of State. Upwards of 12,000 persons were present at this memorial service, which was conducted by the Bishop of Melbourne, assisted by the I.R.C. chaplains, and was practically similar to that held at Hobart. The service closed with the "Dead March" played by the band of the Highland Light Infantry, and the corps returned to their ship. 1901

The *Britannic* was detained until the 30th, awaiting orders, which were delayed owing to a breakdown of the cable; but on the afternoon of that day a message arrived directing the ship to sail the next morning for New Zealand. After a rough voyage the ship anchored off Invercargill early on February the 5th, and at 7 a.m. a Government despatch boat bringing the Premier, Mr. J. G. Ward, and Colonel Penton, the Commandant, and the representatives of the city of Dunedin, came alongside.

Colonel Crole-Wyndham was then informed that arrangements had been made to convey the troops from Invercargill to Christchurch by rail, taking Dunedin on the way. As it was not considered advisable to take the *Britannic* into the harbour, the troops were transhipped with their equipment to the despatch boat, an operation that proved rather tedious on account of the heavy swell running.

At noon the troops disembarked at Invercargill, being received by the local corps on the quay, and were welcomed by Mr. Ward in an eloquent speech.

The corps then marched through the streets to the Queen's Park, where lunch was provided, and as it happened, the officers for the first time heard the toast of "The King" proposed, a circumstance that made a deep impression. After lunch the troops marched back to the station, and entrained in two trains for Dunedin.

Every station on the railway was crowded with people eager to see the trains pass, and at Gore and Milton the troops detrained for a short time and were provided with refreshments by the inhabitants, who welcomed them with the greatest enthusiasm. Finally Dunedin was reached at

1901 11 p.m. and the troops, being detrained, were marched off at once to their respective quarters, being billeted in the town. The next morning the corps paraded in the Triangle and marched through the town, which was gaily decorated for the occasion. After the parade the N.C.O.'s and men were entertained to dinner at the Agricultural Hall, while the officers lunched at the Grand Hotel with the officers of the local Volunteer corps. The weather for the first time proved unpropitious, as the latter part of the march was made in heavy rain, though it cleared up in the afternoon. In the evening an entertainment was given in the Agricultural Hall and the officers dined at the various clubs.

The corps left the next morning at 7.30 a.m. in two trains for Christchurch, stopping en route at Oamoru, Timaru, and Ashburton, at each of which lunch was pressed on the troops by the hospitable inhabitants. Christchurch was reached at 8 p.m., where the corps detrained and marched through crowded streets to the Canterbury Hall, where dinner was provided, after which the troops proceeded by train to Lyttleton, the port of Christchurch, where the *Britannic* lay, and by 11 o'clock they were on board again, after a very exhausting day.

Early in the morning the mounted troops left for Christchurch to take over the horses, which were lent by the local forces, and at 12.30 the rest of the corps left to join them.

The troops marched through the city to the Hagley Park, where they marched past; after which displays were given of sword, bayonet, and lance exercise. Lunch was then partaken of, the Mayor, Sir John Hall, and Mr. Ward being present, and the corps returned in the evening to the ship, which sailed at 7 p.m. for Wellington.

Wellington was reached at 8 a.m. on the 9th. During the morning the officers called on the Governor, Lord

Ranfurley, and on the Premier, Mr. Seddon, whom they 1901 had already met in Australia. At 2.30 p.m. the corps paraded for the march through the city, and formed up after it on the cricket ground, where another display of drills and exercises was given. The men were then entertained to dinner in the Drill Hall by the Mayor and citizens, and the officers at the Club.

The next day was spent quietly on shore, but it was wet, and little could be done in the way of sight-seeing.

On the 11th the corps was divided into two parties, one going to Wanganui to stay the night, the other to Masterton for the day only.

Masterton was reached at 12.30 p.m., where the train was received by the Mayor and the local mounted infantry, most of whom were Maoris. After dinner the visitors were shown a "haka" or Maori war dance, in the Park, and in return the troops gave the usual display of military exercises. The detachment then marched past, and returned in the evening to Wellington. The other party, which had left by an earlier train, arrived at Wanganui at 2.30 p.m., having lunched at Palmerston on the way. The troops, preceded by the local volunteers, marched to the race course, where a great crowd, including many Maoris had assembled, which received them with cheers of welcome. A "haka" and other Maori dances were given, and watched with great interest by the men, after which the National Anthem was sung. An ancient Maori, Major Topia, then made a speech of welcome, after the native custom, and presented the officer in command, Major Askwith, with a fine mat of kiwi feathers for Colonel Crole-Wyndham, and a bunch of huia feathers for himself. Tea was then served under the willow trees, for which the place is noted, by the ladies of Wanganui, and the troops were dismissed to their billets in the town.

1901 The next morning the troops left by train on their return journey, receiving a hearty "send off" from the inhabitants, who seemed to have turned out *en masse* at the station.

The stations on the line were filled with cheering crowds of spectators, particularly at Palmerston, where at least 10,000 people were gathered in the square when the troops arrived.

Here they detrained and marched to the Show grounds, where a military display was given in the presence of a vast crowd of spectators. After lunch the troops again proceeded on their journey, making another stop at Shannon, where a Maori chief presented an historical carved spear, said to be 400 years old, as a Maori offering to Colonel Wyndham.

The ship sailed in the afternoon of the 13th for Napier, which port was reached early the next day. The troops were landed in a Government tender at the Hawkes Bay pier, and after hearing some rather lengthy speeches of welcome, were marched to the Public Gardens, where a dinner was provided. An elaborate "haka" was then performed for the amusement of the visitors, and as soon as it was over Colonel Crole-Wyndham, carrying a ceremonial spear, received the greetings of the Maori chiefs. He was at once robed in a sort of skirt, and a kiwi mat thrown over his shoulders, according to native custom, while spears and feathers were presented to the officers. Colonel Wyndham having conveyed his thanks through an interpreter to the chiefs, the usual military displays were given, which were received with rapturous applause by the assembled multitude, after which the troops marched back through the town to the pier and re-embarked. There were some hopes that the stay of the ship might be prolonged for another day, but orders were received to proceed at once to Auckland, and then to Adelaide.

Early on the 16th the *Britannic* entered the channel leading to Auckland, and by 7.30 a.m. she was berthed alongside of the railway pier. Here, for the last time, the *Dalhousie* was found already anchored. 1901

At 11 a.m. the troops paraded on the quay, horses being provided by the local mounted troops for the cavalry and artillery detachments and the Indian cavalry.

The two contingents marched through the town to the Domain Park, where a large crowd of spectators had already assembled on the wooded slopes surrounding the parade ground. Here they were received by the Mayor, with a short speech of welcome, and also by the indefatigable and omnipresent Mr. Seddon with a much longer one, after which lunch was served in marquee tents.

After lunch the troops gave a military display, which was received with great applause by the spectators, who must have numbered quite 40,000, and in the evening the contingents returned to their respective ships. Leave having been obtained to stay another day at Auckland, arrangements were made to visit Rotorua, the site of the principal hot springs and geysers for which New Zealand is famous. The line passed through a typical New Zealand country (crossing a ridge of mountains on the way, where the incline was so steep that the men actually got out and shoved the train up!) and the changing variety of grassy plain, ferny forest, and volcanic rock proved most interesting.

At 2 p.m. the first train arrived at Rotorua. On the platform were a number of Maoris intheir national dress, who received Colonel Crole-Wyndham with a Maori song.

The troops were escorted to the Spa by a band of Maori girls singing and waving green branches, rather to the embarassment of the men, and after lunch a most interesting and enjoyable afternoon was passed in bathing,

1901 visiting the geysers, and viewing a fine specimen of the old Maori Pah.

On the 19th February the *Britannic* sailed for Adelaide, the capital of South Australia, the departure being delayed by the discovery of a case of scarlet fever among the officers, the unfortunate sufferer, Lieutenant Warrington Morris, having to be hastily landed and conveyed to hospital.

At midnight on the 25th the *Britannic* anchored in Largs Bay, off Adelaide. The Proclamation of King Edward VII had been fixed for the 27th, so the parade was postponed to that day, which gave the troops a welcome rest, as the weather was exceedingly hot, the thermometer marking 100 deg. in the shade.

Early on the 27th the troops were landed in tugs. The cavalry and artillery were, as usual, mounted by the local troop, the household cavalry being provided with grey horses by the police. Many of these animals were quite untrained, and gave a good deal of trouble.

The troops marched through the town to the Exhibition Buildings, where they rested for lunch, the day being very hot and the moist heat most trying. They then proceeded to the Victoria Park, and formed up in two lines on the race track, together with all the local forces.

At 3 p.m. the Governor, Lord Tennyson, drove through the lines of troops, receiving their salute, and then returned to a pavilion that had been erected for the purpose.

The Governor then read the Proclamation of the accession of King Edward, after which the troops marched past and returned to their ship, after a very hot and trying day. There were, indeed, several cases of sunstroke among the men of the I.R.C., and the sufferers had to remain in hospital at Adelaide, though fortunately they were all sufficiently recovered to be able to rejoin before the ship sailed. 1901

The next day was spent in sight-seeing and the usual round of luncheons, dinners, suppers and speech-making, and at midnight the ship sailed for Fremantle.

The I.R.C. was to have attended Proclamation parades at Freemantle and Perth, but on arriving at the former port on March 5th, it was found that there had been several cases of plague there. It being impossible to land the troops, the *Britannic* received orders to return to England, and accordingly sailed on the following day.

The *Britannic* made Colombo on the 17th, where she coaled, and on the 19th sailed for Suez.

Suez was reached on the 30th March, and at 11 a.m. the ship entered the canal. Here the first and only accident of this long and varied voyage occurred, for the *Britannic* ran aground about half a mile from the north outlet of Lake Timsah. There she remained in spite of the efforts of tugs and dredgers till April 5th, and was only got off then after everything moveable had been landed. While the ship was stranded the *Ophir*, outward bound, with the Prince and Princess of Wales, passed.

Major Goddard, who had urgent business in England, left the ship here and went home overland.

After coaling at Port Said, on the 11th, the ship sailed for Malta, arriving there on the 14th. Here a very unfortunate accident happened, for a boat with four of the Cameron Highlanders, who were returning from Valetta, capsized close to the ship. Three of the men were picked up without difficulty, but the fourth, Private Stevenson, somehow got entangled in a rope, and though every effort was made to revive him when he was ultimately recovered, he never regained consciousness.

1901 The ship touched at Gibraltar on the 18th April, taking on board a few officers going home on leave, and arrived at Southampton early on the 22nd April, when the troops disembarked and left by special trains for their several quarters.

Thus ended a most unique and interesting expedition, which must, however, have subjected the interior arrangements of those officers who were fortunate enough to take part in it to some trial, for they ate in Australia and New Zealand eighteen public lunches, and nine State dinners, to say nothing of innumerable breakfasts and suppers, at which Colonel Crole-Wyndham made twenty speeches, thereby earning an undying reputation as a public orator. The heat and excitement proved very trying to the men, at any rate, for with two exceptions every man of the Royal Wilts had been on the sick list at one time or another.

Colonel Crole-Wyndham published an order after landing, in which he referred in very complimentary terms to the uniformly excellent behaviour of the troops.

CHAPTER XXVIII.

The Second Contingent of I.Y.

Towards the end of 1900 the War Office began to realize 1900
the melancholy fact that the war, so far from being over, had only just entered on its most troublesome phase, and that it was likely to go on for an indefinite period unless measures were taken to materially reinforce the worn-out troops in South Africa.

The Imperial Yeomanry had been treated in the vacillating manner usual when money-saving only is in the ascendant. First it was decided to keep the regiments at the front up to their full strength. A stream of recruits were to be sent to the base, and a large Remount Depôt was to be maintained there. Some 400 recruits were indeed sent out at the end of April 1900, but these were earmarked for specified regiments, and as soon as their arrival became known the C.O.'s of corps clamoured to have them sent up at once, which they were. These men were intended to look after the remounts until they and the horses were required to fill casualties at the front; but the horses instead of being kept to meet casualties, had already been used up to mount the men who had come out dismounted.

When Pretoria was taken, the War Office rashly concluded that the war was over; recruiting was summarily stopped, and no more men were enlisted or sent out, the Wiltshire companies so far not having raised any fresh men.

In January 1901, orders were issued to bring all the 1901
regiments of I.Y. up to their full strength by enlisting recruits at their county depôts. But by this time the

1901 regiments in Africa had been reduced to mere skeletons, not only by the unavoidable wastages of the campaign, but because both the officers and men had been encouraged to join the South African police, and all sorts of local corps. Indeed for a short time orders were issued to let any yeoman that wished go home for discharge, if by any chance he got down to the base.*

The regiments too, in pursuance of the extraordinary custom prevalent, had been carefully split up and distributed all over the country in small detachments, so advantage had been taken of this to say that regimental staffs were no longer required, and in the majority of regiments these had been got rid of altogether.

The consequence of these peculiar proceedings was that there were certainly no regiments, and not many companies even, to join at all, and the attenuated remnants of these strenuously objected to being kept away from their private affairs any longer.

The unfortunate and ambiguous wording of the terms of enlistment had already caused great dissatisfaction among the Imperial Yeomen, when the interpretation placed on them by the War Office became known.

The term of enlistment the men subscribed to was stated "to be for one year, or not less than the duration of the war." This the men considered to mean for the duration of the war, or one year at the most, the war then not being expected to last more than a few months. The War Office, however, now not wanting to lose their services, now said that the enlistment was for one year certain, and as long afterwards as the war lasted, no

* On the 6th January 1901, the three companies of the 1st I.Y., then at Harrismith, could only muster eight officers and 121 N.C.O.'s and privates all told; No. 4 having no officers and only eleven rank and file left.

matter how long it went on, though one may be quite 1900
certain that if the war *had* lasted only a few months the men would have been cheerfully discharged without waiting for the end of the year.

Another great source of dissatisfaction was that the I.Y. only got the regular pay of 1s. 3d., while the men of the Colonial forces were drawing 5s. per day. The men did not resent this so much in the case of the oversea Colonials, but they did resent the payment at this extravagant rate of the hordes of worthless ragamuffins that were enlisted at Cape Town, and it did seem rather anomalous that when a man was serving in the I.Y. he should only draw the lesser rate, while the moment he got transferred to a local corps, he began to draw the 5s. a day. Fortunately for the Yeomen, the urgent representations of Lord Roberts were listened to, and from January 1st, 1901, the pay of the N.C.O's and rank and file was raised to the Colonial standard, but the officers, as usual, were left out in the cold, and their pay remained at the old rate, the consequences being somewhat strange; a trumpeter, for instance, receiving more than a second lieutenant. Indeed the pent-up powers of expenditure seem to have burst their restrictions generally about this time, for with the
commencement of the year 1901 the lavish and criminal 1901
waste that characterized the latter part of the war may be said to have begun. Little of this, however, found its way into the pockets of the British combatant officer, whose scanty pay and allowances continued to be subjected to the most rigid scrutiny and the utmost economy.

In January, 1901, orders were issued to prepare drafts to reinforce the I.Y. regiments in South Africa, and on the 21st of that month a regimental order to that effect was issued by Colonel Long. Members of the regiment desirous of enlisting were directed to notify the adjutant to that

1901 effect, and Major Fuller was appointed enlisting officer for the Wiltshire Companies, as Major Bishop was already employed on the same duty at Gloucester.

By the end of February 104 men had been enlisted by Major Fuller, of whom only 10 belonged already to the Yeomanry, and 16 to the Volunteers, after having been tested in riding and put through a course of musketry.

But by this time it had been decided to bring home the remains of the original companies, as it was evidently useless to try and resuscitate them, and to raise an entirely new force. County recruiting was then stopped and those men who were already enlisted were sent to Aldershot, where enlistment generally was being carried on by staff officers appointed for the purpose. Of course, the terms offered at once attracted a vast crowd of all sorts of men, eager to get the pay of 5s. a day, and tempted no doubt also by the innate love of a fight peculiar to the natives of the United Kingdom.

At first the recruiting staff attempted to exercise some discretion by rejecting men who were plainly unfit for service; but they were speedily admonished to the effect that their duty was to enlist men, not to reject them. A similar intimation was even sent to the medical officers who had had the temerity to decline to pass men who were physically unfit. The result was the enlistment of a very motley crew indeed, the great majority being absolutely ignorant of any species of drill, unable to ride, and of course totally unacquainted with the use of a rifle.

No proper arrangements either had been made at Aldershot to receive the large number of recruits that presented themselves, particularly considering the season of the year, and the county contingents were greatly disgusted at the unnecessary hardships they were compelled

to undergo, as well as at the class of men they were 1901
compelled to associate with.

Had there been time to teach these new yeomen riding and musketry and even the merest rudiments of drill, no doubt, after weeding out those who were glaringly incapable, they would have made good enough soldiers, but both the time and the means were wanting for this.

The officers too, particularly in the lower ranks, were, in the majority of cases, just as untrained and inexperienced as the men they commanded, many of them having never worn uniform until they received their yeomanry commissions. Over the doings of this very strange force, when it did get to the front, history had better be silent.

The Wiltshire recruits, however, were more fortunate than the majority of the county recruits, inasmuch as they did at any-rate join what was left of the old 1st I.Y. The remnant of the 63rd Company was added to those of the 1st regiment that elected to remain in Africa, and they had the advantage of being commanded by Sir Thomas Fowler, who remained also. They did some useful work in the second part of the campaign, particularly in one instance, at Drahoek on July 8th, 1901, where a detachment under Corporal Townshend beat off a determined attack when surrounded by a large force of the enemy, killing the Boer Commandant. Corporal Townshend, who was wounded, was promoted Sergeant by Lord Kitchener for his conduct in this affair.

The Wiltshire Companies also had the misfortune to lose Sir Thomas Fowler, who was killed in action on April 20th, 1902, under the following circumstances.

The 1st regiment I.Y. (now composed, of course, of the second contingent), was at Brindisi on the 18th April, 1902. Information was received that 50 Boers were living at a farm near Moolman's Spruit, about 15 miles off.

1902 Lieut.-Colonel Perceval, who was then in command, marched in the evening of the 19th with 160 men under Major Davies and Sir T. Fowler, intending to surprise the enemy. The farm was reached at 1 a.m. on the 20th, but it was bright moonlight, and the enemy, who were very much stronger than was reported, were on the alert and expecting an attack, having fully prepared the farm for defence.

Having surrounded the farm buildings, the whole force advanced in extended order to the attack, and on getting within 200 yards, were received with a hot fire. Sir Thomas, who showed, as usual, the greatest intrepidity, led his party to within 20 yards of the house, when he fell, shot through the right thigh.

The attack was repulsed with considerable loss, and when the medical officer, who remained behind to attend to the wounded, found Sir Thomas, it was too late, for that gallant and unfortunate officer had died from loss of blood, the artery having been severed by the bullet.

His body was afterwards brought in and was buried at Ficksburg.

APPENDIX TO CHAPTER XXVI.

ROLL OF THE SECOND CONTINGENT.

Ashman, W. J.
Burrows, W. (Yeo)*
Butler, W. G. (Vol.)
Blount, F. W.
Baldwin, A. T. W.
Bourton, C. W.
Bridges, B.
Clarke, H. C. (Yeo.)
Crowther, G. (Yeo.)
Currie, E. H.
Collingbourne, B.
Clements, G. T. (Vol.)
Collis, W.
Collett, W.
Douglas, S. (Yeo.)
Davies, J. C. (Yeo.)
Dewey, C.
Duck, E.
Disten, A. C.
Duncan, E. G. (killed in action).
Davies, G. (died)
Davis, H. J.
Fox, C. A.
Godfrey, G. B.
Gough, F.
Green, W. G.
Harraway, B. (Yeo.)
Hunt, J.
Hay, H.
Hawkins, T. H. T.
Hewlett, Wm.
Haddrell, D.
Hodgson, C. E.
Hughes, F. J.
Harvey, E. R. (died).
Jukes, C.
Jones, J. (died)
Jefferies, W.
Kemp, W. J. (Vol.)
Keeling, E. E. (died).
Lenton, W. G.
Lewis, O. G. (Vol.)
Lapham, A.
Leavey, H. G. (Vol.)
Lambeth, F.
Lem, F. R. F.
Lewington, E. J.
Lodge, E.
Leworthy, G.
Miles, W. G.
McIntosh, H. (Vol.)
Moxham, W. (Vol.)
McCarthy, D. (killed in action).
O'Hare, W. J. (died)
Peters, W. J. H.
Powis, C. W. (Yeo.)
Perkins, T.
Purnell, A. H. (Vol.)
Pelly, W. J. (Vol.)
Park, F. C.
Pickford, W. F. (Vol.)
Prigge, A. J.
Parsons, R. E. V.
Prigge, G. E.
Perry, W. (died)
Ruddle, C. W. (Vol.)

Randell, F.
Righton, F. L. (Vol)
Russ, A. L. (Vol.)
Rutt, F. R.
Rich, W. A. (Vol.)
Snow, M. (Yeo.)
Snell, A. J.
Sparks, A. E.
Sadler, A.
Stainer, T. R.
Strong, E. (Vol).
Stephens, R
Smelt, A. H. (died)
Smith King, J. (Yeo.)
Sims, A. C. W. (died).
Smith, F.
Townsend, T. (Yeo.)
Thatcher, S. (Vol.)
Townsend, A.
Townsend, J. T.
Townsend, J.
Thomas, C. O. (killed in action).
Temperton, J. H. (died).
Wycherley, R. A.
Watts, F. H.
Wallridge, R.
Williams, F.
Wilkins, W. F. J.
Whale, H.
Winter, J.
Wicks, W.
Westbury, T. H.
Wheeler, J. S.
Wood, C. H.

* (Yeo.) signifies that the man was a Yeoman, and (Vol.) a Volunteer, previous to enlistment.

CHAPTER XXIX.

The Re-Organization of the Yeomanry.

The year 1901 proved an epoch in the history of the 1901
yeomanry cavalry, for it marked a total change in public opinion as to its usefulness, and an earnest attempt on the part of the Government to realize the aspirations of its members and to make it a really effective part of the defences of the State.

For many years the yeomanry cavalry had been rather tolerated on account of its antiquity than considered really useful, and looked on merely as a sort of costly plaything. Jokes at the expense of the yeomen appeared from time to time in the comic papers, not it is to be feared sometimes altogether undeserved, and the force had one or two narrow escapes from total abolition.

The country did not, in fact, take the yeomanry seriously, and the natural consequence followed that the yeomanry did not take themselves seriously either. Smartness in turn out, well-groomed horses, punctuality, and knowledge of drill, were not expected of a yeoman; their services in bye-gone years had faded out of remembrance, and the period of training was regarded as an expensive but enjoyable outing.

The author, indeed, can well remember the dismay with which he witnessed his first regimental parade. It was, to begin with, quite an hour after the time mentioned in orders before the last of the 200 or so troopers, out of a nominal 400, who thought it worth while attending had leisurely strolled on to parade, while the appearance of the clothing, saddlery, and accoutrements, all ill-fitting and in the last stages of decay, was enough to make the least sensitive of adjutants weep.

1901 But this was not at all the fault of the men themselves. They had never been taught any better ; they had never been expected or invited to be any smarter or more punctual, had indeed never had any chance of being so ; and when the ridiculously short period of what was facetiously styled "permanent duty", namely a nominal eight days that left only really four for instruction, is taken into account, when they did get the chance, their improved appearance and greatly increased efficiency in the field was most remarkable.

Fortunately, owing to many reasons, not the least being the support and encouragement afforded to the yeomanry by *H.R.H. the Prince of Wales, and by H.R.H. the Duke of Cambridge when Commander-in-Chief, the force not only avoided extinction altogether, but made, in spite of the lack of encouragement in quarters that ought to have known better, a great and progressive improvement both in general efficiency and appearance which extended over some twenty years before the late war put it to the proof, though the depression in agriculture had a most disastrous effect on its numbers.

But now for the first time for nearly a century the country was forced to look seriously to its defences. The thinly-veiled hostility of every nation in Europe, kept in check merely by a well-grounded fear of the British Fleet, and the total inability of the Regular Forces of the Crown to cope successfully with the obstinate resistance of the two Boer Republics, brought home to everyone the necessity of a complete re-organization of the Auxiliary Forces, while the invaluable, the even indispensable, assistance so generously afforded in the time of need, caused the force to be recognised at last as what it was, the only possible reserve for the inadequate cavalry of the

* Now King Edward VII.

line, and thus at last the yeomanry cavalry emerged 1901
triumphant from its long ordeal of neglect.

In the autumn of 1900 a committee was appointed by the War Office to consider the question of the re-organization of the yeomanry, and to make recommendations. This committee consisted of seven members, namely: Viscount Galway, the Earl of Dundonald, the Marquis of Bath, Sir John Dickson-Poynder, and Colonels Rolleston and Lucas.

The committee made its report on the 2nd January, 1901, and proposed many important changes in the constitution of the yeomanry cavalry. The chief of these were:—

1. That regimental adjutants should be restored.
2. That the permanent staff should be increased.
3. That there should be a regimental quartermaster.
4. That the Army Act should apply to yeomanry during the training.
5. That the training should take place in camp.
6. That permanent duty should extend over eighteen days, of which it should be compulsory to attend fourteen, and that musketry should be practised locally, or

   That the permanent duty should be for twenty-one days, of which seventeen should be compulsory, and that the musketry instruction should be given during the training.
7. That pay should be given during attendance at musketry.
8. That the pay should be at the rate of 10s. per day, with £5 horse allowance extra.
9. That there should be a staff officer at the War Office to represent the yeomanry.
10. That there should be a yeomanry decoration for long service and good conduct.

1901 11. That the yeomanry should be armed with a rifle and bayonet, and that if no swords were to be used, then with a revolver in addition.

This last recommendation and the question as to whether the yeomanry should be cavalry or mounted infantry caused considerable discussion, and the committee were divided on the point, the Marquis of Bath, Lord Galway and Colonel Rollestone being in favour of their remaining cavalry, while Lord Dundonald and Sir John Dickson-Poynder recommended that they should be mounted infantry.

There was also considerable difference of opinion among the O.C.'s. of regiments on this point when the decisions of the committee were submitted to them, Colonel W. H. Long in particular holding very strongly that they should remain cavalry, on the ground that it was their original and proper function, and that to turn them into mounted infantry would be most unpopular and a serious check to recruiting in the county.

Much, no doubt, may be said in support of either view. A large body of infantry must have cavalry to render it really effective, and owing to our very short supply of regular cavalry it is certain that in case of mobilization the yeomanry would have to act as the cavalry to the Volunteers' divisions.

On the other hand the short training that the yeomanry get can hardly be sufficient to make them really efficient cavalry in the field, whereas it can make them the best of mounted infantry, and they did excellent service in that capacity during the Boer War.

Owing to the peculiar conditions of the war in South Africa the value of mounted infantry has received rather exaggerated recognition, but no one can say what the result of attempting to apply such large bodies of mounted men in any European war would be. There would certainly be difficulties in disposing of so many horses in an enclosed country. The question of cavalry versus mounted infantry therefore will have to stand over until it can be subjected to the test of actual experience under other conditions than those that characterized the late war. One would have thought at any rate that the most casual consideration of the war would have brought home to anybody both what *could* be done by an efficient force of cavalry and what could *not* be done without one. 1901

The general failure of the regular cavalry to accomplish any striking success was brought about by causes quite beyond the control of the cavalry officers themselves. There were no cavalry officers of any standing on the general staff, and consequently the cavalry was both often not used when it should have been, and, still more often, given by *infantry officers quite ignorant of anything appertaining to horse flesh, tasks that it was impossible for any cavalry to perform. With the exception of General French, none of the cavalry leaders were of any high standing in the army, and were in consequence not given a free hand in the field; and, lastly, the regular cavalry was not only miserably insufficient in numbers for the duties it should have performed, but suffered also from the scanty supply of remounts, which was totally inadequate to keep the regiments efficient in the field.

The brilliant exploits of General French in the operations about Colesberg, and in the relief of Kimberley, showed what cavalry could do under a capable general who was allowed a free hand, while in the latter part of the war, when the Boers themselves began to act as cavalry, their repeated and in many cases successful charges on

* General Macdonald was a noticeable offender in this respect.

1901 horseback showed what a resolute body of mounted men could accomplish in the absence of an opposing cavalry force.

Lord Methuen's force was overwhelmed at Tweebosch by a charge of mounted Boers, tactics frequently repeated with success by Delarey, while an even still more instructive action took place at Roodeval on April 11th,
1902 1902, where 1,500 mounted Boers charged the British column under Kekewich in line.

Miserably mounted as they were, on ponies that could hardly raise a canter, these men actually rode to within 300 yards of the British line before they turned, in the face of the fire of 1,500 rifles supported by 6 guns.

According to infantry theorists they should have been mowed down by hundreds, but it is a melancholy fact that they effected an unmolested retirement with the trumpery loss of 80 men killed and wounded.

Can it be doubted that if these men had been well mounted they would have rolled up the British line, or that if Kekewich had possessed a single regiment of regular cavalry the Boer horsemen would not have been cut to pieces in their retreat.

The early victories of Lord Methuen, too, were thrown away because his weak and ill-mounted cavalry could not follow up the defeated enemy, and the same thing occurred at Talana, where the Boers effected an unmolested retreat; while after the relief of Ladysmith another great chance was thrown away because the infantry staff could not bring itself to let loose the cavalry brigade on the confused mass of guns and wagons that was struggling at the foot of the mountain passes, and which, greatly to the surprise of the Boers themselves, was allowed to effect a tardy and unmolested escape.

In short, the South African campaign, so far from

proving regular cavalry to be useless in modern warfare, 1901
demonstrated clearly that with an efficient cavalry under a capable and resolute leader a general could accomplish the most impossible feats, while without it, though he might remain victor on the field of battle, his victory would bring him no decisive gain.

The recommendations of the committee were duly considered by the War Office, and eventually Army Order 109 was issued. This was published in Regimental Orders on the 2nd May, 1901. It effected such a sweeping and important change in the constitution of the yeomanry cavalry that its provisions, at least the chief of them, are inserted as under.

1. The title of Yeomanry Cavalry is changed to that of Imperial Yeomanry.
2. The brigade organization is abolished, regiments are to have four squadrons with full regimental staff and a gun section.
3. Any regiment whose numbers fall below 420, or any squadron below 100 enrolled and efficient members for two consecutive years is liable to be abolished.
4. Those officers and men are classed as efficient on the 1st October each year who during the previous twelve months—(*a*) attended not less than 14 complete days permanent duty exclusive of marching in and marching out; (*b*) performed the prescribed number of drills; (*c*) completed the prescribed musketry drills and practice, and passed into the 2nd class, bandsmen (4 per squadron), clerks, artificers and regimental staff excepted.
5. Rates of pay to be as follows per day :—Sergeant, 8s. 2d.; Corporal, 7s. 6d.; Trumpeter, 5s. 8d.; Private, 5s. 6d.
6. Ten dismounted men per squadron are allowed.

1901 7. Marching pay is granted according to the yeomanry regulations.

8. Forage allowance of 1s. 6d. per day is granted for training and squadron drills.

9. Horse allowance of £5 is granted to each yeoman unprovided with a Government horse for each full training.

10. Pay of 3s. per day for three days is allowed for attendance at musketry instruction, with travelling allowance of not more than 6s.

11. The contingent allowance is fixed at £3 per year for each efficient yeoman, or £5 for the first year for each recruit needed to bring a regiment up to its new strength.

12. £20 per annum allowed for each squadron store, and £30 for the head-quarter store.

The Secretary of State in addition issued the following instructions :—

1. The annual training to take place at any date between May 1st and September 30th, to last over 16 days, exclusive of the two extra days allowed by the regulations.
2. Sword exercise abolished.
3. Recruits to attend 12 drills, other yeomen 6 drills.
4. Rifles, bayonets, and sets of saddlery to be found by the Government.
5. 100 rounds of ball cartridge per man to be provided.
6. Karkee coat, cord pants, gaiters or putties, hat and spurs to be found out of contingent allowance.
7. The establishment is fixed at 596 of all ranks, inclusive of 30 officers, an adjutant, and 5 permanent sergeants, with 1 officer and 16 N.C.O.'s and men for a gun detachment.

This was indeed a far-reaching and sweeping change in

the organization of the yeomanry. There were not wanting 1901
many pessimists who predicted confidently that it would be impossible to get men to join in sufficient numbers under these new and stringent conditions. These gloomy forebodings were entirely falsified. The change to mounted infantry passed unnoticed; the training under canvas so materially lessened expenses that many men were able to join who had been previously debarred by the want of the money necessary for living in quarters during permanent duty; the horse allowance caused quite a new source to be drawn on in enabling townsmen who could ride, but who were not able to keep horses, to enlist into a mounted force; and lastly, the more business-like adjuncts of the training generally silenced completely those who had been in the habit of sneering at the yeomanry as soldiers *pour rire.* No difficulty whatever was experienced in finding an ample supply of men, not only to fill up the new establishment of the existing corps, but to raise many entirely new regiments also; and the new era was everywhere welcomed with the utmost enthusiasm by both officers and men.

CHAPTER XXX.

1901.

1901 On the 15th January Colonel W. H. Long published the following order relative to the retirement of Major Bishop:—

"The C.O. desires to express in orders his hearty appreciation of the services which have been rendered to the regiment by Major Bishop during the five years of his adjutancy, and the regret which he, in common with the officers, N.-C.-O.'s, and men of the regiment, regard the termination of his service with the Royal Wiltshire Yeomanry."

Captain Collins, from the Scots Greys, was gazetted adjutant, vice Major Bishop, on the 22nd May, the Brigade system, whereby one adjutant served two regiments, having been now abolished.

On the 21st February memorial services were held in many of the parish churches in memory of those Imperial Yeomen who had died in South Africa, these being now twenty-nine in number.

On the 9th May the regiment provided an escort for Field-Marshal Earl Roberts from Salisbury to Bulford, on the occasion of his opening a bazaar at the latter place in aid of the Soldiers' Home, and on the 12th a letter was received from the Field-Marshal conveying his thanks, together with some complimentary remarks about the turn-out of the men and horses.

The return of the Wiltshire companies from Africa being expected in July, great preparations were made throughout the county to give them a fitting welcome. On the 8th July the *Roslyn Castle* arrived at Southampton, bringing 48 of the 1st Company, under command of Lieutenant Henderson. The Company arrived at

Chippenham by train on the following day, where they 1901
were welcomed by the Mayor and Corporation and a large number of the townspeople. The troops were first marched to the parish church, where a thanksgiving service was held, the address at the close being given by the Rev. Canon Rich, after which they were entertained at a banquet in the Town Hall. At Swindon, the men belonging to that district were also received by the Mayor and Corporation, together with four companies of the Volunteers with their band, and at Devizes the townspeople gave the eight men belonging to the town a most enthusiastic welcome.

On the 18th Captain Speke and Lieutenants Thornton, Awdry, and Speke arrived at Chippenham with 12 of the 2nd Company, and were received like their predecessors by the Mayor and Corporation, and entertained to dinner.

The returning yeomen generally met with hearty welcomes locally, and the Warminster men were received at Maiden Bradley by the Duchess of Somerset, who presented each with a valuable gift as a souvenir of the occasion.

On the 26th July a parade of the returned I.Y. was held on the Horse Guards Parade, in London, at which His Majesty himself presented the Queen's medal for South Africa to a selected number of officers and men.

The Wiltshire companies were represented by 120 N.C.O.'s and men, under command of Lieutenants Henderson and Awdry.

The troops, some 3,000 in number, were formed up by companies on the ground, and passed in single file before the King, who personally presented each man with his medal. After the parade the Wiltshire men adjourned to the Westminster Palace Hotel to dinner.

On the 10th August a banquet was given to the

1901 returned Imperial Yeomen by the county. This, by permission of Sir J. Dickson-Poynder, was held in the Old Riding School at Hartham Park, the chair being taken by Colonel W. H. Long, as High Sheriff, in the unavoidable absence of the Lord Lieutenant, the Marquis of Lansdowne, from whom a letter of apology was received and read. There were present 82 of No. 1 Company, 72 of No. 2 Company, and 70 of the 63rd Company. Many of the past and present officers of the regiment attended, and many also of the leading gentlemen of the county.

After several interesting speeches and the usual loyal toasts, the High Sheriff presented their medals to those of the men who had not been able to attend the King's parade. Games and various entertainments then took place in the Park, and in the evening the guests left by special train from Corsham.

The regiment assembled for permanent duty on the 1st September, and went into camp at Perham Down. The new regulations had proved an excellent stimulus to recruiting, no less than 134 new members having joined during the year, bringing the total strength up to over 400.

On the 12th, for the second time, the regiment was exercised in field firing, which was made more realistic by being conducted under a "general idea".

The regiment marched to Beacon Hill, when the scouts reported a party of the enemy, with 2 guns, in position on Milston Down. The squadrons were then ordered to attack, dismounted, in succession.

On the 14th the painful news of the assassination of President McKinley arrived. A telegram of condolence was despatched on behalf of the regiment to the American Ambassador, who sent a reply of thanks.

The inspection, which was made by Major-General

Grant, C.B., took place on the 18th, and on the day following the regiment was dismissed. 1901

All ranks were greatly interested to hear of the brilliant success of Colonel Scobell, Scots Greys, a former adjutant, by the capture of Lotter and his entire commando in the Cape Colony on September 5th, and a telegram congratulating that gallant officer was at once despatched to him in the name of the regiment.

This commando was one of the most active and mischievous of those that were then at large in Cape Colony, whose activity, coupled with the mountainous and difficult country they were operating, seemed to defy all attempts to destroy them.

Colonel Scobell was in command of a detachment of 200 men made up of the 9th Lancers and Cape Mounted Rifles. Not the least difficulty the troops had to contend with in dealing with them arose from the enemy generally being able to obtain the most accurate information beforehand of their intended movements from their sympathizers among the Dutch farmers of the colony. Colonel Scobell, however, was this time too clever for them.

Having ascertained the locality where the Boers were laagered for the night, he halted at the place they had occupied the previous day without disclosing his intentions to anyone.

After dark a sudden order was issued to the troops to mount, and after making a circuitous march of 25 miles, Colonel Scobell came on the laager on the further side before daybreak.

The bulk of the sentries had been posted on the side the British were supposed to be. A small picquet only was met with, the men of which were at once shot down, and the laager was surrounded before the enemy realized what had happened.

1901 After enduring a heavy fire for some time, a white flag was hoisted, but a too eager lancer, who rode up to receive the expected surrender, was treacherously shot. The fire was then recommenced, and only ceased when the Boer leaders came out and surrendered, when the whole commando laid down their arms after losing 19 men killed and many others wounded.

Colonel Scobell's victory was complete. In addition to Commandants Lotter and Breedt he took four field cornets, 104 prisoners, 240 horses, and 25,000 rounds of ammunition, being practically the entire commando. For this smart bit of work Colonel Scobell received the C.B. direct from the King.

Lotter and Breedt, who were both Cape rebels and had been guilty of several atrocious murders in the course of their career in the Colony, were both tried by court-martial afterwards and most deservedly executed.

Indeed, this brilliant little action was a marked contrast to the ill success that attended the usual efforts to bring these marauding commandos to bay. The few regular troops that could be spared for service in Cape Colony were worn-out by a year's hard campaigning, while the local levies, by which it was sought to supplement them, were a great deal worse than no use at all. All the local men that were of any value had long ago gone to the front. The wretched crew that were now enlisted were tempted merely by the extravagant rates of pay offered to them. Many of them were rebels at heart, none of them had the smallest military training; few of them had the least intention of risking their skins in a fight. They were worse than useless because they served merely as a means of supplying the Boers with horses, arms, and ammunition when captured.

The following report of Smuts, one of the most able

and active of the Boer generals still at large, is interesting 1901 as throwing a lurid light on the situation. It fell by accident into the hands of the British authorities, and, being written for the confidential information of his own government, there is no reason to doubt its strict accuracy, and it discloses a state of things that certainly did not occur when the first contingent of Imperial Yeomanry had matters in hand:—

"I left the Transvaal on August 1st. 340 men and four commandants joined me on the Wet River, in the Hoopstadt district, by the end of the month It took one month to get through Orangia. We had to evade seven columns, each from 500 to 1,000 strong, and to get through tho line of blockhouses on the Modder River."

After describing at length the difficulties he encountered in getting into the Cape Colony, giving his losses at 10 killed, 14 wounded, and 30 taken prisoners, in the second week of September Smuts states that he was safely lodged in the Bamboo Mountains, near Tarkastad, in the south-east of the Colony, with 200 men, the rest having been sent away in detachments. The diary then runs as follows:—

"14th September. Left the mountains through the Eland's River Poort. Found the pass occupied by the 17th Lancers, whom we attacked, killing and wounding 73, and taking 50 prisoners. An Armstrong gun and a Maxim were taken and destroyed. Captured also two wagon-loads of ammunition and rifles, and 300 horses and mules, with the loss of one killed and five wounded.

"Then started for Maraisburg Was surrounded, but got through towards Graham's Town. Lost 100 horses in crossing the mountains. The pursuit was so keen we had to cross over into Zuurberg on the 29th September.

"2nd October. Followed by Gorringe and the Defence Force of Somerset East, while the Defence Forces of Alexandria and Uitenhage were in our front. Another column was on our right, and the mountains, the passes of which were held, was on our left. Attacked and took a pass, killing one and taking 13 prisoners.

1901 "3rd October. Retired on Zuurberg. Half-way up off-saddled in Kloof. Gorringe's column came up. Attacked them at once. Enemy lost 200 killed and wounded and 700 horses. There were no Boer casualties.

"4th October. Crossed mountains to the north, sent Bower towards Graaf Reinet separately, forage being scarce

"6th October. Attacked by Defence Forces of Alexandria and Graham's Town. Captured both their camps, killing 10 and taking 30 prisoners, with 70 horses. No Boer casualties. Started after Bower, who had met the same day 100 of the Somerset East Defence Force, and Springvalle, killing some and taking 20 prisoners, with a number of horses. Bower then moved into the Candeboo mountains, where he met with a 'check' by the East Somerset Defence Force.

"13th October. Van de Venter and Kirsten were at Doornbusch, where they were attacked by a Defence Force. We took 210 prisoners and 250 horses, with the loss of three wounded. They then went to Sandys River, where they were attacked by Colonel Lukin, and lost one killed, one wounded, and 10 taken prisoners on the 21st October.

"Van de Venter and Kirston then went to Calvinia, capturing 17 of the Victoria Defence Force and 19 of the Fraserburg Defence Force, and defeating Caldwell and the 5th Lancers at Brands Kraal, killing and wounding 10, taking 30 prisoners and many horses.

"Bower was in the Candeboo mountains pursued by Colonel Scobell. He was joined by the remains of Scheeper's commando, and traversed Van Rynsdorp.'

Smuts then summarizes his proceedings thus:—

"On the 4th September we started operations with 200 men, and up to the end of November lost four killed, 16 wounded, and 35 taken prisoners. The British lost 732 killed and wounded, 439 taken prisoners, one gun and one maxim, a large quantity of ammunition, and 1,136 horses during the two months we were in the Colony."

Thus these 200 men ramped about Cape Colony with comparative impunity for two months, devastating the farms of the loyalists, ill-treating the loyal natives in the most brutal manner, and generally paralysing all trade. Smuts' account gives a very good sample of the doings of

these commandos, of which there were several others at 1901
large in the Colony at the time.

The utter worthlessness of these town guards and local defence forces was so plainly demonstrated, however, by these proceedings, that they were disarmed and dismissed. Smuts, himself, afterwards transferred his attentions to Namaqualand, where he collected upwards of 2,000 men, and terrorized the whole district up to the end of the war, though a large force was sent by sea from Cape Town to Port Nolloth to deal with him.

The behaviour of the so-called "defence forces" was in many cases so disgraceful that all reports of these actions described by Smuts were censored out of existence, and it is impossible to know whether his accounts of the losses sustained by them is correct or not. His account of the defeat of the 17th Lancer squadron is not only quite accurate, as far as it goes, but actually understates the losses, both of killed and wounded, and in prisoners. The official reports give the strength of the Boers in this affair as 700! Whereas by this account they did not exceed 200 at the most.

CHAPTER XXXI.

1902-1903.

The new Militia and Auxiliary Forces Act passed in
1902 August, 1901, had been an important change in the status of the officers of the yeomanry, and as the Act could not affect those who had obtained their commissions previous to its being passed, this resulted in the creation of two classes of officers.

To obviate this inconvenient state of things, the War Office, in January 1902, issued an appeal to the old officers inviting them to resign their original commissions, and to receive in exchange fresh ones under the new Act, retaining of course their former rank and seniority; and this was accordingly done by all the officers of the Royal Wilts who were affected.

By another W.O. Order all officers who had served with the Imperial Yeomanry in Africa were made eligible for the reserve of officers.

On the 3rd March the Prince and Princess of Wales arrived at Chippenham from London on their way to visit the Duke of Beaufort at Badminton.

Their Royal Highnesses were received at the station by the Mayor and a Guard of Honour of the Volunteers, and were escorted by a travelling escort of the Royal Wiltshire as far as the boundary of the county, where it was relieved by the Gloucester Hussars.

* In April the news was received of the death in Africa of Sir Thomas Fowler, the only one of the original officers of the Wiltshire companies of the Imperial Yeomanry who had remained with the second contingent.

The long postponed ceremony of the Coronation of King Edward VII took place on August 9th this year. This,

* V, p. 147.

as was the case on the occasion of the Diamond Jubilee, 1902
was attended by detachments from the Imperial Yeomanry. The Royal Wilts sent a detachment made up of picked men from the several troops consisting of 1 regimental sergeant-major, 1 sergeant, and 24 rank and file under command of Lieutenant Thornton.

The detachment was quartered in buildings and sheds of the Great Western Railway at Paddington. As before the men paraded on the Horse Guards Parade, and were posted at the same place in the Mall, but with their backs to Marlborough House.

After the ceremony the detachment returned home by train. Lieutenant Thornton and Sergeant G. Moore received the coronation medal.

The regiment this year assembled for permanent duty at Bulford on the 1st September, there being present 491 of all ranks, including 28 officers, out of an enrolled strength of 561. This was only six below the full strength of the new establishment, and made the regiment the fourth strongest corps in the service.

Field firing was again carried out during the training, and included practice with the machine guns.

On the 24th September the regiment was inspected by Major-General Lord Chesham, Inspector-General of Imperial Yeomanry, there being 486 of all ranks on parade out of a total strength of 525.

On the 31st October General Lord Methuen was entertained by the Mayor and Corporation of Devizes at a public reception in honour of his services during the Boer War. This was followed by a banquet at which the Marquis of Lansdowne presided. The Royal Wiltshire provided a travelling escort for the gallant general on the occasion, made up entirely of men who had served in South Africa.

The new badges of rank were taken into wear this year.

1903 On the 14th March, 1903, Major the Marquis of Bath was promoted to be second in command *vice* Goddard retired.

This year it was again decided to hold manœuvres in Wiltshire, and Colonel Long applied for permission to take part in them.

The 31st August had been fixed on for the regiment to assemble for the training, which was to take place in camp on West Down. The manœuvres were to commence on the 14th September, and the War Office, after first saying it was impossible for the regiment to attend them at all, then suggested that the old soldiers only should go, leaving the recruits, of whom there were 150, in camp.

To this Colonel Long pointed out several objections; the difficulty was avoided by altering the marching-in day to the 26th August, so that the regiment could leave for the manœuvres after the inspection, which was fixed for the 10th September.

The War Office, which institution seemed determined to make things as unpleasant as possible all round, then proposed to post the regiment to the first army corps, whereas it properly belonged to the second. After some correspondence this was altered, and a promise with difficulty extracted that the regiment should be kept together and not split up; but by way of a final rebuke for over-zealousness, a request for the supply of water-bottles and other equipment was flatly refused. The regiment accordingly went into camp on West Down on the 26th August and was inspected by Major-General Baden-Powell on Thursday, the 10th September, there being present 554 of all ranks out of an enrolled strength of 597, the establishment now being complete.

The weather had been very stormy and threatening for some days, and the inspection was scarcely over when the wind rose to regular tempest accompanied by a drenching downpour of rain. The camp suffered severely, 1903 the mess marquees, canteen and officers' mess tents, cook houses, and many bell tents being blown down, and the troops on the march to join the 2nd army corps passed a most miserable night.

Owing to the delays and obstructions that had been placed in the way, it proved impossible at the last for the whole regiment to take part in the manœuvres, and volunteers were called for. Two strong squadrons were formed under command of Colonel W. H. Long, with the Marquis of Bath as second in command, and on Saturday, the 12th September, these marched to Corsham to join the 2nd army corps.

The two squadrons were formed into a provisional yeomanry regiment made up to four squadrons by a squadron of the Gloucester Hussars, a troop of the Glamorgans and a troop of the Devonshire yeomanry. This was attached to the cavalry brigade under command of Colonel Lowe.

The "general idea" was that the enemy (Blue) had gained temporary command of the sea, and projected an invasion of England. Meanwhile two raiding forces were landed to create a diversion pending the landing of Blue's main army somewhere on the south coast. This was expected to take place about the 19th September.

One of these raiding forces had attempted a landing on the east coast, but had failed. The other had effected a landing in the Bristol Channel and taken Bristol. Meanwhile the British army is being mobilized and held in readiness to meet the expected main invasion.

Blue's "special idea" was

On the morning of the 13th September his camps were on the line Corsham—Holt, with a cavalry brigade on the line Devizes—Calne—Sutton Benger.

1903 His spies report two divisions at Aldershot, and a force between Aldershot and Petersfield, with a detached brigade with guns and cavalry at Chipping Norton. His orders are to seize Reading and to pretend a march on London so as to draw of Red's attention from the south coast. Blue has no base, his transports having left Bristol, Swindon is full of stores and munitions belonging to the Red army.

The "War" began at midnight, Sunday the 13th. The Blue army was composed of two divisions, the 5th under General Sir Leslie Rundle, the 6th under General Sir C. Knox, with the usual corps troops and a cavalry brigade of three regiments and six R.H.A. guns, with a supply depôt at Westbury.

The Red army, under General Sir John French, also consisted of an army corps of two divisions with a cavalry brigade under General Scobell, and at the commencement of the operations was encamped at Petersfield, while the "detached" brigade, under General Bruce Hamilton, belonging to the Red force was in the neighbourhood of Wantage.

On the morning of the 14th the Blue army marched in the direction of Reading. The cavalry brigade was sent on to seize Swindon, which it did without opposition, Marlborough was also occupied early in the morning, and by the evening the Blue army held the Vale of Pewsey to Swindon as far as Aldbourne, the 5th division being at Calne, the 6th at West Overton.

At midnight on the 13th the Red cavalry brigade left the camp at East Meon, for Newbury, a distance of 45 miles.

Newbury was occupied at 10.30 a.m., a halt of half-an-hour only having been made at Whitchurch during the march, by two regiments and six R.H.A. guns, one regiment having been detached to occupy Andover.

Patrols were pushed out at once to Wantage to get into 1903 touch with General Bruce Hamilton, and to Kintbury and Hungerford. Meanwhile the infantry divisions marched to Avington, near Winchester, where they encamped for the night.

On the 15th fighting commenced, General Wood sent a cavalry regiment to seize Hungerford, but at noon this was attacked by General Scobell with his whole brigade and promptly driven out. The 5th division was then ordered to retake the place, and the Red cavalry had to make a hasty retreat in its turn.

At night the positions were as follows :—

Blue army—5th division at Froxfield and Hungerford; 6th division and corps troops at Ramsbury; cavalry brigade at Lambourne. Red army—General Bruce-Hamilton and the cavalry brigade at Newbury, covering the passages over the canal; General French with two infantry divisions and corps troops at Kingsclere, 5 miles south-east of Newbury.

On Wednesday morning Blue moved the 6th division and corps troops to Lambourne Down, taking up a strong position which he proceeded to entrench, the 5th division moving meanwhile from Hungerford towards Shefford to cover this operation.

Red moved his whole force from Newbury towards Shefford, marching along the Lambourne Valley. The opposing forces came into contact about 10 a.m., General Rundle's division had to bear the brunt of the attack of the whole Red army as the brigades came successively into action, being supported only by the distant artillery fire from Lambourne Down, and was gradually forced back from Shefford. Late in the afternoon "Cease fire" was sounded by Lord Roberts, who acted as umpire-in-chief. The two armies were directed to camp in the positions

1903 they then occupied, and to resume the action the next morning.

On Thursday morning at 10 a.m. General French renewed his attack on the 5th division, forcing General Rundle to retire on Eastbury Down, which was held by the rest of the Blue army, prolonging his right at the same time by deploying the 1st division and sending the cavalry still further on the extreme flank.

At 2 p.m. Blue delivered a counter attack with his whole force, sending his cavalry to turn Red's right flank. But the turning movement of Red's cavalry had not been seen, and Blue's cavalry, after having been rather shattered by the fire of the guns of the 1st division, was charged in flank by General Scobell as it came into the open, and cut to pieces.

The result of the fighting on this part of the field of battle was that Blue's left was completely turned by the flanking movement, and when "cease fire" sounded and the manœuvres came to an end, his counter-attack was held to have failed, partly for that reason, and partly owing to the heavy loss the fifth division must have sustained in the two days fighting.

General French was therefore adjudged the victor, as it was held impossible for Sir Evelyn Wood to continue his march on Reading under the circumstances.

Some further adverse criticisms were passed on that general's want of energy in not having attempted to crush General Bruce-Hamilton's brigade before it joined hands with the 1st army corps, or at least for not having tried to prevent the junction of the two forces; for not having made more effective use of his cavalry; and for the very insufficient strength of the party detached to seize and remove the stores at Swindon.

The manœuvres were rather unsatisfactory to the Royal

Wiltshire, as no use was made of them at all during the first two days they lasted, and but little on the third day. 1903

This year a chaplain was appointed to the regiment, after a lapse of nearly 100 years since the retirement of his predecessor, in the person of the Rev. W. L. Waugh, vicar of Chiseldon.

The following regimental order was afterwards issued by Colonel W. H. Long :—

"CHIPPENHAM,
3rd October, 1903.

"The Officer Commanding desires to express to all ranks of the regiment under his command his profound satisfaction at the way in which the work was performed during the Training, and also at the soldier-like and un-complaining manner in which the unfortunate climatic conditions were borne.

"He feels sure the regiment will not soon forget that they had the privilege to be next to the famous Brigade of Guards.

"The Officer Commanding also desires to say how gratified he was by the strength of the two squadrons which he was able to take to the Manœuvres, thanks to the patriotic action of those who volunteered. He desires to call the attention of all ranks to the following paragraph, which is taken from the Order issued to the two Army Corps by Field-Marshal Earl Roberts, Commander-in-Chief.

"' 5. The Imperial Yeomanry, who showed their soldierly spirit by volunteering to take part in the Manœuvres, also did good work and proved that they had greatly benefited by the training of the past three years.'

"He desires also to express his own satisfaction at the way in which the difficult and novel duties connected with Manœuvres were performed, and he is confident that many valuable lessons were learned which will be of great benefit to the regiment in the future.

"By order,
"W. F. COLLINS, Major and Adjutant,
"Royal Wiltshire Imperial Yeomanry."

In 1903 the regiment lost the distinction of possessing the yeoman with the longest service in the United

1903 Kingdom by the retirement of Squadron-Sergeant-Major Parrott.

Mr. Parrott had been for many years the Quartermaster of the Warminster troop, and was made Squadron-Sergeant-Major on the reorganization, after having declined the post of Regimental Quartermaster.

T. H. 5TH MARQUIS OF BATH.
Colonel 28th April, 1906.

CHAPTER XXXII.

1904-1907.

In 1904 the "cutting down" process began again to be 1904
applied to the Auxiliary Forces. On the 16th March an Army Order reduced the establishment of all regiments of Imperial Yeomanry by 120 men, reducing it from 596 to 476. The establishment of officers was not altered.

In March, Captain Collins vacated his appointment as Adjutant. He was succeeded by Captain H. J. Tilney, 14th Hussars, who was gazetted on April 1st. This year it was decided to revert to the old custom of having the annual training in the spring instead of the autumn, this being found generally more convenient to everyone. The regiment accordingly assembled this year at Swindon on the 16th May, and went into camp at Burderop Park.

On June 2nd the regiment was inspected by Colonel Smithson, there being 564 of all ranks on parade out of a total strength of 602, and was dismissed the following day.

On December 31st an Order was issued notifying that the King had been pleased to approve of the words "South Africa, 1900-01" being borne on the colours and appointments of the Royal Wiltshire Imperial Yeomanry in recognition of the services of the three Wiltshire Companies in South Africa during the Boer War.

On February 4th, 1905, a monument was unveiled in 1905
Salisbury Cathedral in memory of the officers and men of the several Wiltshire corps who lost their lives in the course of the Boer War.

Representatives of the Regular and Auxiliary Regiments of the County were present at the ceremony, to-

1905 gether with most of the members of the County Council, the Mayor and Corporation of Salisbury, who attended in State, and a great number of interested spectators. After an impressive service, which was conducted by the Dean, the monument was unveiled by the Marchioness of Lansdowne in the absence of the Marquis, the Lord Lieutenant of the County, who was prevented by illness from being present himself.

The Memorial consists of a large panel of copper on which is mounted an inscription with the names in enamel on silver-gilt, headed by those of the four officers and 44 N.C.O.'s and men of the three Wiltshire Companies who died or were killed during the war.

In 1905, the regiment assembled for permanent duty on the 21st May, at Uffington, where it went into camp. Col. Long being on leave most of the time, Lord Bath commanded in his absence.

This year the King approved of silver medals being issued to those men of the Imperial Yeomanry who had served continuously for a period of 10 years without missing a single day of permanent duty.

These well-earned decorations were presented by Colonel Long after church parade, on Sunday, June 4th, to the following members of the regiment:—

Regimental Sergt.-Major E. Morel.
" Quarter-Master-Sergt.-Major W. Freegard.
Squadron Quarter-Master-Sergeant J. E. Ashby.
" " " " F. W. Austin.
" Sergt.-Major A. Balch.
" " T. Candy.
" " T. B. Craxton.
" " A. G. Duffosee.
" " J. Moore.
Sergeant C. Fox. Sergeant J. Hiscocks.

Sergeant G. Hobbs. Sergeant J. Hulbert. 1905
„ W. Marshman. „ H. Parsons.
„ G. Slade. „ G. Chinn.
„ E. Smallbones. „ E. Ellis.
Corporal W. Hunt. Private H. J. Morris.
„ J. Duck.

The regiment was inspected by Colonel T. C. Porter, Staff Officer for I.Y., there being 422 of all ranks on parade out of a total strength of 473.

In April, 1906, Colonel W. H. Long retired from the 1906
service, and the same day issued the following order:—

"The Officer Commanding, in relinquishing the command of the regiment, desires to thank all ranks for their loyal support and zealous co-operation, without which it would have been impossible to carry out smoothly and successfully the many changes which have been effected in the regiment during the period of his command.

"The Yeomanry system has undergone a complete reform, the result of the War, which imposed so severe a strain upon the nation, and led to the demand for Yeomen to serve at the front. The O.C. rejoices to remember that the Royal Wilts, whose motto by right of service is 'Primus in Armis' was second to none in the enthusiasm and loyalty which responded to the country's call. The service companies rendered gallant service in South Africa, and though many officers and men gave their lives for their Sovereign and Country, the deep regret felt for their loss is tempered by the glorious reflection that they shed lustre on the old corps of which they were such devoted members.

"The regiment has more than held its own, and the Commanding Officer feels sure that the officers, non-commissioned officers and men will ever strive, by self denial and devotion to duty to maintain the high standard of efficiency which he is proud to know exists at the present. With profound regret the Officer Commanding resigns the command which has been to him a source of great pride and happiness, and bids his old comrades good-bye and a hearty God-speed."

Major and Hon. Lieut.-Colonel the Marquis of Bath was promoted to be Lieut.-Colonel to command *vice*

1905 Colonel Long retired, and on the 7th May he issued the following Regimental Order :—

"The Commanding Officer takes this opportunity of expressing the sincere regret of the whole of the Royal Wiltshire Yeomanry that Colonel the Right Honourable W. H. Long has given up the command. All ranks are sensible of the debt of gratitude owing to him for the eminent services he rendered to the regiment at a critical period in its history, and their warmest wishes for his future welfare accompany him in his retirement."

Colonel W. H. Long had indeed rendered eminent services to the regiment on more than one critical period. By raising the strong troop at Rood Ashton in 1876-7, he probably saved the corps from extinction, as the number of members was getting perilously near the point when it would have been liable to disbandment under the new regulations, thanks to the depression in agriculture and the extremely unsympathetic attitude of the War Office towards the Yeomanry Cavalry.

Colonel Long's prompt and energetic action with regard to the raising and training of the three Wiltshire Service Companies at Trowbridge is, of course, fresh in everybody's recollection, and largely contributed to the very satisfactory result of showing that the Royal Wilts was still *Primus in Armis*.

1906 In 1906, the regiment assembled for permanent duty at Wantage, on May 22nd, where it went into camp in conjunction with the Berkshire Imperial Yeomanry, Lord Bath being in command.

The two regiments did not drill together, and only met when they formed opposite sides in the practice of outpost duty and reconnaissance.

The regiment was inspected by Colonel T. C. Porter, C.B., Staff Officer for I.Y., on the 4th June, there being 427 of all ranks on parade out of a total strength of 453, being

23 under the establishment, and on the following day the troops were dismissed. 1906

In April, 1907, Captain Tilney completed his term of service as Adjutant, and on the 13th, Captain B. Ritchie, 15th Hussars, was gazetted Adjutant in his place. 1907

This year the regiment met for permanent duty at Warminster, on the 13th May, Lord Bath being in command, and went into camp at the foot of the Downs just outside the town.

The inspection, by Colonel Hegan, Staff Officer for Imperial Yeomanry, took place on the 27th May, there being present 418 of all ranks, out of a total strength of 443, this being 33 under the establishment. The troops were dismissed on May 30th. The weather this year was unusually cold and cheerless.

At the end of the training, Colonel Long was formally presented with a Muster Roll of the regiment, beautifully engrossed and illuminated on vellum in a silver-mounted frame.

On the 20th July the regiment provided a Field Officer's escort for the King on the occasion of His Majesty's visit to Bowood. The squadron, which was under command of Major Fuller, met His Majesty at the Chippenham Railway Station. In addition to the squadron, a special personal escort, consisting of fourteen officers, under command of Colonel The Marquis of Bath, was in attendance on His Majesty.

The year 1907 was remarkable for the introduction by Mr. Haldane, Secretary of State for War, of an entirely new scheme of national defence.

By this scheme, which came into operation in 1908, the old County Associations that were in existence during the wars with the French Emperor Napoleon were reconstructed, and to these the whole management of the Aux-

1907 iliary Forces, now styled the Territorial Army, was entrusted. This necessarily entailed many changes in the organization of the yeomanry, the chief of which were as follows:—

The designation of "Imperial" was omitted from the title of the yeomanry. The establishment of yeomanry regiments was fixed at 25 officers, including an extra Major as second-in-command, and an extra Lieutenant to command the gun section, and 449 Warrant Officers, N.C.O.'s and men.

The County mounted troops were divided into Brigades, the Royal Wilts forming the South-Western Mounted Brigade, with the North Somerset and Hampshire Yeomanry, a battery of Horse Artillery, a Field Ambulance, and a Supply Company, all volunteers.

The scale of pay for privates in the yeomanry was fixed at 1*s.* 2*d.* a day, with 1*s.* extra messing allowance, and free rations. The horses were to be found by the Association if needed; £5 horse allowance being paid to those yeomen who brought their own horses for the whole training of 15 days, 6*s.* 8*d.* being deducted for each day less.

An equitation grant of £1 per head was granted to each yeoman certified an efficient horseman.

The training to be for 15 days, attendance at eight being required for a certificate of efficiency.

The capitation grant was abolished, all equipment and clothing being provided by the County Association out of moneys supplied by the War Office.

The yeomanry and other territorial forces to be subject to military law while embodied.

* The term of enlistment to be for four years. Discharges to be bought for £5, subject to three month's notice.

* Or as the County Association shall decide. In Wiltshire one year's enlistment is accepted.

Officers and men of existing corps to be transferred to 1907
the territorial force by their own consent only, such consent to be signified before the 30th June 1908.

No Warrant Officer or N.C.O. over 55, or Corporal or Private over 45 years of age to be accepted.

In 1908, the regiment assembled for permanent duty 1908
on May 27th, and went into camp at Shepherd's Shore, five miles from Devizes. There were present 384 of all ranks out of a total strength of 392, 58 men in addition, who had not yet decided whether to re-engage under the new organization, being absent on leave, the time for their final decision not expiring until June 30th.

The regiment was inspected by Major-General Scobell, C.B., on the 5th and 6th of June, and dismissed on the 10th.

This being the last training under the old organization, and an entirely new system having been now inaugurated, commencing from the 1st July 1908, the author begs to take leave of his readers, if they have not already taken leave of him, by wishing the regiment a long and prosperous career under the new conditions of service, and that it may ever continue in the future as in the past

PRIMUS IN ARMIS.

APPENDIX I.

THE OFFICERS OF THE WILTSHIRE YEOMANRY. 1884—1908.

REGIMENTAL STAFF.

Colonels and Lieut.-Colonels.

J. A. Marquis of Bath, Hon. Colonel of Regiment, 14 Nov., 1890.

H. C. K. Marquis of Lansdowne, K.G., Hon. Colonel of Regiment, 24 Feb., 1897.

G. Sotheron-Estcourt, promoted Lieut.-Colonel Commanding from Major and Hon. Lieut.-Colonel, 14 Nov., 1890.

W. H. Long, promoted Lieut.-Colonel Commanding from Major and Hon. Lieut.-Colonel, 23 March, 1898.

T. H. Marquis of Bath, promoted Lieut.-Colonel Commanding from Major and Hon. Lieut.-Colonel, 28 April, 1906.

Majors, Second in Command.

G. Sotheron-Estcourt, promoted Major from Captain and Hon. Major, 28 Dec., 1886.

W. H. Long, promoted Major from Capt. and Hon. Major, 12 Dec., 1890.

T. H. Marquis of Bath, Major and Hon. Lieut.-Colonel, to be second in command, 18 Mar., 1903.

G. L. Palmer, Major and Hon. Lieut.-Colonel, to be second in command, 27 July, 1906.

Adjutants.

H. J. Scobell, Captain 2nd Dragoons (Scots Greys), 9 October, 1889, *vice* Aylmer.

C. Bishop, Capt. 9th Lancers (Brigade Adjutant), 1 July, 1895, *vice* Scobell.

W. F. Collins, Capt. 2nd Dragoons, 22 May, 1901, *vice* Bishop.

H. J. Tilney, Capt. 14th Hussars, *vice* Collins, 1 April, 1904.

B. Ritchie, Capt. 15th Hussars, 13 April, 1907, *vice* Tilney.

Surgeons.

G. T. K. Maurice, Surgeon-Lieut., *vice* Surgeon-Lieut.-Colonel J. B. Maurice resigned, 6 April, 1893.

O. C. Maurice, Surgeon-Lieut. 10 Sept., 1895.

Veterinary Surgeons.

F. P. Bennett, appointed Veterinary-Lieut. 30 Jan., 1892.

T. V. Pettifer, Veterinary-Lieut. 13 March, 1895.

E. E. Seldon, Veterinary-Lieut. 29 Aug., 1906.

Chaplains.

W. L. Waugh, The Rev., 27 May, 1903.

ALPHABETICAL LIST OF OFFICERS, JOINED, PROMOTED AND LEFT, 1884-1908.

Astley, H. F. L., Capt., resigned 20 April, 1886, with Hon. rank of Major, and permission to wear uniform.

Awdry, C. S., Gent., 2nd Lieut. 23 April, 1898; temp. Lieut. in Army, 7 Feb., 1900; Lieut. (seconded) 13 June, 1900; Hon. Lieut. in Army, 20 Aug., 1901; Capt. 1 Aug., 1903.

Awdry, R. W., Gent., 2nd Lieut. 5 March, 1902.

Aylmer, H. L., Capt. 16th Lancers, Adjutant; vacated appointment 9 Oct., 1889.

Bath, J. A., Marquis of, Col., Hon. Col. of Regiment, 14 Nov., 1890; died, 20 April, 1896.

Bath, T. H, Marquis of (Viscount Weymouth), Capt. and Hon. Major; to be Major 17 Aug., 1901; second in command, 18 March, 1903; Hon. Lieut.-Colonel, 14 March, 1902; Lieut.-Colonel and Hon. Col. to command, *vice* Long, retired, 28 April, 1906.

Benett-Stanford, J. M., late Lieut. 1st. Dragoons; Lieut. 17 Dec., 1892; resigned 1900-1.

Bevan, E. H., gent., 2nd Lieut. 2 Nov., 1901; resigned 1902-3.

Bennett, F. P., gent., Vet.-Lieutenant 30 Jan., 1892; resigned 1895.

Bishop, C., Capt. 9th Lancers; Brigade Adjutant 1 July, 1895; vacated 21 May, 1901.

Bruce, Lord F. C. Brudenell, Capt., to be Hon. Major 20 May, 1891; resigned 18 May, 1898.

Browne, M. Meredith, Lieut., resigned 5 March, 1886.

Calley, T. C. P., Capt., resigned 8 June, 1888.

Cardigan, J. W. J. C., Earl of, Lieut. 13 Feb., 1897; Lieut. (supernumerary) 6 April, 1898; Capt. 3 Sept., 1898; resigned 1900; transferred to 11th Hussars.

Clutterbuck, H., Lieut., resigned 3 March, 1888.

Curtis, T. R., Lieut., resigned 6 Feb., 1895.

Cox, E. R., 2nd Lieut. 11 July, 1900; Lieut. 29 Aug., 1903

Collins, W. F., Capt. 2nd Dragoons; appointed Adjutant *vice* Bishop 22 May, 1891; vacated appointment March, 1904.

Deacon, T. H., Gent., 2nd Lieut. 11 Aug., 1900; Quartermaster 13 July, 1901; Hon. Captain 19 Oct., 1901.

Dickson-Poynder, Sir John, Bart., Lieut., resigned 2 April, 1887; rejoined 2nd Lieut. 8 Jan., 1890; Capt. 7 Dec., 1898; temp. Lieut. in army, 7 Feb., 1900; Hon. Lieut. in army, 5 Feb., 1901; Major 31 May, 1902; resigned 1908.

Estcourt, G. Sotheron, Capt., Hon. Major 7 May, 1886; Major 28 Dec., 1886; Hon. Lieut.-Colonel 15 April, 1887; Lieut.-Colonel to command 15 Nov., 1890; Hon. Colonel 14 Nov. 1893; resigned 8 March, 1898.

Faber, W. V., Capt., retired R. Artillery, to be Lieut. 15 Aug., 1901; Capt. 6 June, 1902; resigned 1903-4.

Fair, T. H., Gent., 2nd Lieut. 16 July, 1902; resigned 1904-5.

Folkestone, W. Viscount, Capt., resigned 2nd July, 1886.

Folkestone, J., Viscount, 2nd Lieut. 21 June, 1889; resigned 1900-1.

Fowler, Sir Thomas, Bart., 2nd Lieut. 2 Feb., 1892; Lieut. 1 May, 1895; temp. Lieut. in army 7 Feb., 1900; Capt. (seconded) 17 Aug., 1891; killed in action S. Africa, 20 April, 1902.

Finlay, D., Gent., 2nd Lieut. 10 Sept., 1904; resigned 1905.

Fuller, J. M. F., Lieut., to be Capt. 6 April, 1898; Major on establishment 17 Aug., 1901; Asst. Adjutant 3rd brigade 18 July, 1900.

Fuller, W. F., Gent., 2nd Lieut. 13 June, 1900; Lieut. 24 May, 1902; Capt. 3 May, 1906

Fuller, Robert F., Gent., 2nd Lieut. 13 June, 1900; Lieut. 22 April, 1903.

Goddard, FitzRoy Pleydell, Lieut. (supernumerary) 2 Oct., 1880; Capt. 7 Sept., 1888; Major 3 Oct., 1900; resigned 1903-4.

Goldney, G. Prior, Lieut, to be Capt. 13 Dec., 1890; Hon. Major 23 Jan., 1892; resigned 1898-9.

Gouldsmith, C. E., Gent., 2nd Lieut. 24 Feb., 1897; resigned 13 June, 1900.

Grant, S. C., Gent., Lieut. 26 May, 1902.

Grove, Sir Thomas F., Bart., Major and Hon. Lieut.-Colonel; resigned 3 Dec., 1886.

Gwatkin, J. R. G., Gent., 2nd Lieut. 4 May, 1887; Capt. 25 May, 1889; Major 17 Aug, 1901; resigned 4 June, 1902.

Hankey, B. H. A., Gent., 2nd Lieut. 20 Aug., 1902.

Henderson, A., Gent., 2nd Lieut. 27 Aug., 1904.

Helme, B., Capt., died 2 Sept., 1893.

Hulse, E. H, Lieut., Capt. 2 July, 1886; resigned 20 Aug., 1887.

Joicey, J., Gent, 2nd Lieut. 6 May, 1891; Lieut. 1 May, 1895; Capt. 3 Oct., 1900; resigned 1905-6.

Kelk, Sir J. W., Bart., Capt., resigned 18 April, 1894.

Kingscote, E., Gent., Assistant Surgeon 17 March, 1894; Surgeon-Lieut. 17 March, 1894; Surgeon-Capt. 17 May. 1899; resigned 1900-1.

Lamb, B., Gent., 2nd Lieut 2 Nov., 1891.

Lansdowne, H. C. K., Marquis of, K.G., Hon. Colonel of regiment 24 Feb., 1897.

Lopes, H. T. (Lord Ludlow), 2nd Lieut. 5 Dec, 1888; resigned 1 March, 1895; rejoined 2nd Lieut. 13 June, 1900, Lieut. 26 March, 1902; Capt. 24 Sept., 1903; resigned 8 March, 1907.

Long, W. H., Capt., Major 13 Dec., 1890; Hon. Lieut.-Colonel and second in command 13 Dec, 1890; Lieut.-Colonel to command 23 March, 1898; resigned April, 1906.

Long, R. Chaloner C., Gent, 2nd Lieut. 26 June, 1895; resigned 5 May, 1897.

Maurice, J. Blake, Surgeon-Lieut.-Colonel, resigned 6 May, 1893.

Maurice, G. F K, Gent., Surgeon-Lieut. 9 May, 1892; resigned 1903-4.

Maurice, O. C., Gent., Surgeon-Lieut. 10 Sept., 1895; Surgeon-Capt. 29 Aug., 1900.

Mackay, G. E., Gent., 2nd Lieut. 4 April, 1894; Lieut. 7 Dec., 1898; Capt. 17 Aug., 1901; Major 3 May, 1906.

Mann, W. H., Gent., 2nd Lieut. 16 July, 1902.

McNiven, E., Gent., 2nd Lieut. 23 April, 1898; resigned 1901-2.

Methuen, Hon. P. A., 2nd Lieut. 18 Oct., 1905.

Miles, F. F., Lieut., resigned 10 Feb., 1888.

Miles, A. E., late Capt. 60th Rifles, Lieut. 8 April, 1890; resigned 18 April, 1894; rejoined 23 Jan, 1895, as Capt; Hon. Major 24 Nov., 1897 (Assistant Adjutant 3rd Yeomanry Brigade 23 Jan., 1895); resigned 24 Aug., 1901.

Meux, Sir H. Bruce, Bart., Capt. and Hon. Major, to be Major and Hon. Lieut.-Col. (supernumerary) 7 Dec., 1898; died 12 Jan., 1900.

Neeld, Sir A. W., Bart., Capt. and Hon. Major, to be Major 6 April, 1898; Hon. Lieut.-Colonel; died 11 Aug, 1900.

Palmer, G. L., Gent., to be Lieut. 27 April, 1885; Capt. 2 Sept., 1893; Major 17 Aug., 1901; Hon. Lieut.-Colonel and second in command 27 Aug., 1906.

Palmer, M. G. L., Gent., 2nd Lieut. 14 March, 1906.

Pelly, Sir H., Bart., 2nd Lieut. 2 April, 1887; resigned 4 May, 1892.

Pettifer, T. V., Gent., Vet.-Lieut. 13 March, 1895: resigned 1906.

Poore, R. A., Gent., 2nd Lieut. 11 Feb., 1893; Lieut. 7 Dec., 1898; Capt. (supernumerary) 17 Aug., 1901.

Poynder, Dickson, *v.* Dickson-Poynder.

Ritchie, B., Capt. 15th Hussars, to be Adjutant *vice* Tilney, 13 April, 1907.

Sadler, J. N., Lieut.; resigned 22 June, 1888; Hon. rank of Captain and leave to wear uniform.

Scobell, H. J., Capt. Scots Greys, to be Adjutant *vice* Aylmer, 9 Oct., 1889; vacated appointment 9 Oct., 1894.

Seldon, E. E., Gent., Vet.-Lieut. 29 Aug., 1906.

Spenser, H. E., late Lieut. 13th Hussars; Lieut. 18 Jan., 1899; resigned 28 Jan., 1905.

Smith-Bingham, H. B. B., Gent., 2nd Lieut. 5 Feb., 1900; Lieut. 17 Aug., 1901; resigned 10 March, 1902.

Stancomb, John F., Gent., 2nd Lieut. 15 April, 1889; Lieut. 16 Jan., 1892; resigned 1901-2.

Sutton, A. G., Gent., 2nd Lieut. 4 May, 1887; Lieut. 16 Jan., 1892; resigned 1894-5.

Tilney, H. J., Capt. 14th Hussars, to be Adjutant *vice* Collins, 1 April, 1904; vacated appointment April, 1907.

Thornton, C. M., Gent, 2nd Lieut. 5 May, 1897; temporary Lieut. in Army 7 Feb., 1900; Lieut. (seconded) 13 June, 1900; Capt. 22 April, 1903. (Hon. Lieut. in Army 27 June, 1901.)

Thynne, Lord Alexander G., 2nd Lieut. 14 April, 1897; temp. Lieut. in Army 7 Feb., 1900; Lieut. (seconded) 13 June, 1900; Capt. 22 April, 1903. (Hon. Lieut. in Army 28 July, 1902.)

Thynne, U. O., late Lieut. Rifle Brigade, to be Capt. 31 May, 1902; Major 22 April, 1903.

Watson-Taylor, G. S. A., Lieut., to be Capt. 28 Dec., 1886; resigned 25 Jan., 1889.

Waugh, W. L., Rev., to be Hon. Chaplain 27 May, 1903.

Weymouth, T. H., Viscount, Capt. 2 Sept, 1893, *vide* Bath, Marquis of.

Yeatman-Biggs, W. H., Gent., 2nd Lieut. 5 April, 1902; resigned 1905-6.

APPENDIX II.

LIST OF REGIMENTAL PRIZE WINNERS, 1885—1908.

1885.

Regimental Prize, Swordsmanship·—Trooper R. Butler, Marlborough.
Best Troop :—Rood Ashton.
Best Recruit :—Trooper F. Collins, Rood Ashton.
Challenge Cup, Musketry :—Trooper Baily, Rood Ashton.
Best Score :—Sergeant-Major Carpenter, Malmesbury.
Best Average Attendance :—Salisbury and Warminster, tie.

1886.

Regimental Prize, Sword:—Trooper J. E. Ashley, Rood Ashton.
Best Troop :—Rood Ashton.
Best Recruit :—Trooper H. Sims, Rood Ashton.
Challenge Cup, Musketry :—Trooper Ashley, Rood Ashton.
Lowest Percentage 3rd Class Shots :—Warminster.
Best Attendance :—Salisbury.

1887.

Regimental Prize, Sword :—Trooper R Butler, Marlborough.
Best Recruit :—Trooper J. E. Cole, Marlborough.
Challenge Cup :—Trooper Johnson, Devizes.
Lowest Percentage 3rd Class Shots :—Warminster.
Best Attendance :—Salisbury.

1888.

Regimental Prize, Sword :—Trooper W. Sloper, Swindon.
Best Recruit :—Trooper Ashton, Chippenham.
Best Troop :—Rood Ashton.
Challenge Cup, Musketry :—Trooper Johnson, Devizes.
Lowest Percentage 3rd Class Shots :—Warminster.
Best Attendance :—Warminster.

1889.

Regimental Prize, Sword :—Sergeant Sloper, Swindon.
Best Troop :—Rood Ashton.
Best Recruit :—Trooper J. Hussey, Chippenham.
Lowest Percentage 3rd Class Shots :—Salisbury.
Best Attendance :—Salisbury.

1890.

Regimental Prize, Sword :—Sergeant Ashby, Rood Ashton.

Best Troop :—Rood Ashton.

Best Recruit :—Trooper D. Jones, Malmesbury.

1891.

Regimental Prize, Sword :—Trooper Austin, Chippenham.

Best Troop :—Rood Ashton.

Challenge Cup, Musketry :—Sergeant Godwin, Malmesbury.

Lowest Percentage 3rd Class Shots :—Swindon.

Best Attendance :—Rood Ashton.

1892.

Regimental Prize, Sword : —Trooper Austin, Chippenham.

Best Troop :— Rood Ashton.

Best Recruit :—Trooper W. Ruddle, Rood Ashton.

Challenge Cup, Musketry :—Trooper Balch, Swindon.

Lowest Percentage 3rd Class Shots :—Salisbury.

Best Attendance :—Warminster.

1893.

Regimental Prize, Sword :—Corporal F. Austin, Chippenham.

Best Troop :—Rood Ashton.

Best Recruit :—Trooper Hamley, Devizes.

Challenge Cup, Musketry :—

1894.

Regimental Prize, Sword :—Corporal Austin, Rood Ashton.

Best Troop :—Rood Ashton.

Best Recruit :—Trooper Mortimer, Rood Ashton.

Challenge Cup, Musketry :—Sergeant Ashby, Rood Ashton.

1895.

Regimental Prize, Sword :—Sergeant Ashby, Rood Ashton.

Best Troop :—Rood Ashton.

Best Recruit :—Trooper Butcher, Warminster.

Challenge Cup, Musketry :—Trooper H. Passmore, Swindon.

1896.

Regimental Prize, Sword :—Trooper Hillier, Marlborough.

Best Recruit :—Trooper Bailey, Warminster.

Best Troop :—Rood Ashton.

Challenge Cup, Musketry :—Corporal A. Balch, Swindon.

1897.

Regimental Prize, Sword :—Sergeant J. Moore, Malmesbury.

Best Troop —Rood Ashton.

Best Recruit :—Trooper S. Rawlings, Rood Ashton.

Challenge Cup, Musketry :—Corporal Carpenter, Chippenham (shot for at Warminster).

Best Average and Attendance :—Rood Ashton, full attendance; no 3rd Class Shots.

1898.

Regimental Prize, Sword :—Sergeant Sudweeks, Devizes.

Best Troop :—Rood Ashton.

Best Recruit :—Trooper J. Butler, Devizes.

Challenge Cup, Musketry :—Corporal Balch, Swindon (shot for at Trowbridge).

1899.

Regimental Prize, Sword :—Trooper G. Butcher, Warminster.

Best Recruit :—Trooper E. Wyatt, Salisbury.

Challenge Cup, Musketry :—Trooper A. Duffosee, Warminster.

1900.

Regimental Prize, Sword :—Trooper Johnson, Devizes.

Best Recruit :—Trooper Johnson, Devizes.

Best Squad :— Devizes.

Challenge Cup, Musketry :—Trooper Harding, Malmesbury.

1901.

Challenge Cup, Musketry :—Sergeant A. Duffosee, Warminster.

1902.

Challenge Cup :—Sergeant A. Duffosee, Warminster.

1903.

Challenge Cup :—Corporal H. D. Bathard, Rood Ashton.

1904.

Challenge Cup :—Corporal H. D. Bathard.

1905.

Challenge Cup :—Corporal H. D. Bathard.

Corporal Bathard, having now won this Cup three years in succession, became entitled to keep it. The Commanding Officer therefore presented him with a silver replica of it. This seems to have been the first time the challenge cup was won three years in succession by the same person, since it was presented by Lord Ailesbury in 1864, though on several occasions it was won two years running.

1906.

Challenge Cup :—Corporal C. F. V. Fenton, Malmesbury Troop.

1907.

Challenge Cup :—Corporal C. F. V. Fenton.

APPENDIX III.

EXPENDITURE IN RAISING THE THREE COMPANIES OF WILTSHIRE IMPERIAL YEOMANRY.

RECEIPTS.

	£	s.	d.
Contingent Fund (I. Y. Committee)	30,888	8	3
Messing and Forage do . ..	2,373	7	5
County Fund	7,119	13	5
Galloping Gun Fund (County)*	1,897	8	0
Officers' Commissariat (South Africa) Fund (County)*	500	0	0
Insurance (No. 2) Fund (County)*	1,155	3	6
(The 1st Insurance was paid from the County Fund.)			
	£43,934	0	7

EXPENDITURE.

	£	s.	d.
Equipment of Men	5,542	13	7
Do Horses (Saddlery, Shoes, Rugs, etc.) ..	6,686	14	1
Purchase of Horses	18,081	10	0
Men's Messing at Trowbridge	1,308	8	5
Forage for Horses at Trowbridge	1,106	5	9
Barrack Accommodation	376	16	11
Temporary Stabling	1,564	15	5
Stationery, Printing, and Advertisements	220	4	4
Railway Carriage, Brake Hire, and Haulage	459	14	9
Medical Fees	166	13	9
Galloping Guns and Carriages	1,957	13	6
Insurance of Men	3,561	8	11
Officers' Mess (South Africa). (This was for the whole of the 1st Battalion and the 63rd Co.) ..	1,275	15	2

* Specially raised.